The Early Modern Englishwoman:
A Facsimile Library of Essential Works

Series II

Printed Writings, 1641–1700: Part 2

Volume 2

Alicia D'Anvers

The Early Modern Englishwoman:
A Facsimile Library of Essential Works

Series II

Printed Writings, 1641–1700: Part 2

Volume 2

Alicia D'Anvers

Selected and Introduced by
Robert C. Evans

General Editors
Betty S. Travitsky and Anne Lake Prescott

ASHGATE

Published by
Ashgate Publishing Limited
Wey Court East
Union Road
Farnham
Surrey, GU9 7PT
England

Ashgate Publishing Company
110 Cherry Street
Suite 3-1
Burlington
VT 05401-3818
USA

Ashgate website: http://www.ashgate.com

British Library Cataloguing-in-Publication Data
D'Anvers, Alicia
    Alicia D'Anvers. - (The early modern Englishwoman : a
    facsimilie library of essential works. Printed writings
    1641-1700, series 2 ; pt. 2, v. 2)
    I.Title II.Evans, Robert C.
    821.4

Library of Congress Cataloging-in-Publication Data
The early modern Englishwoman: a facsimile library of essential works. Part 1. Printed writings, 1641–1700/general editors, Betty S. Travitsky and Anne Lake Prescott.

Library of Congress Control Number: 2003105826

The image reproduced on the title page and on the case is from the frontispiece portrait in *Poems. By the Most Deservedly Admired Mrs. Katherine Philips* (1667). Reproduced by permission from the Folger Shakespeare Library, Washington, DC.

ISBN 978-0-7546-3094-4

Transferred to Digital Printing in 2010

Printed and bound in Great Britain
by Printondemand-worldwide.com

CONTENTS

PREFACE
BY THE GENERAL EDITORS

Until very recently, scholars of the early modern period have assumed that there were no Judith Shakespeares in early modern England. Much of the energy of the current generation of scholars has been devoted to constructing a history of early modern England that takes into account what women actually wrote, what women actually read, and what women actually did. In so doing the masculinist representation of early modern women, both in their own time and ours, is deconstructed. The study of early modern women has thus become one of the most important—indeed perhaps the most important—means for the rewriting of early modern history.

The Early Modern Englishwoman: A Facsimile Library of Essential Works is one of the developments of this energetic reappraisal of the period. As the names on our advisory board and our list of editors testify, it has been the beneficiary of scholarship in the field, and we hope it will also be an essential part of that scholarship's continuing momentum.

The Early Modern Englishwoman is designed to make available a comprehensive and focused collection of writings in English from 1500 to 1750, both by women and for and about them. The three series of *Printed Writings* (1500–1640, 1641–1700, and 1701–1750) provide a comprehensive if not entirely complete collection of the separately published writings by women. In reprinting these writings we intend to remedy one of the major obstacles to the advancement of feminist criticism of the early modern period, namely the limited availability of the very texts upon which the field is based. The volumes in the facsimile library reproduce carefully chosen copies of these texts, incorporating significant variants (usually in appendices). Each text is preceded by a short introduction providing an overview of the life and work of a writer along with a survey of important scholarship. These works, we strongly believe, deserve a large readership—of historians, literary critics, feminist critics, and non-specialist readers.

The Early Modern Englishwoman also includes separate facsimile series of *Essential Works for the Study of Early Modern Women* and of *Manuscript Writings*. These facsimile series are complemented by *The Early Modern Englishwoman 1500–1750: Contemporary Editions*. Also under our general editorship, this series will include both old-spelling and modernized editions of works by and about women and gender in early modern England.

New York City
2003

vii

INTRODUCTORY NOTE

The few facts known about D'Anvers are admirably surveyed by Germaine Greer et al. (pp. 376–77), who rely partly on an annotated copy of *Academia* once owned by Anthony a Wood. D'Anvers was born Alice Clarke, daughter of Samuel Clarke, once a 'superior Beadle of Law in Oxfordshire' and also the university's 'first … director of printing'. These facts help explain D'Anver's intimate familiarity with Oxford and especially with the workings of the press. Alicia was christened as 'Alice' in 'Holy Cross Church at Holywell on 5 January 1668' – less than two years before her father's death. Sometime before 23 December 1690 she married Knightley Danvers (born in 1670), 'the son of Daniel Danvers, an Oxford graduate practising as a physician in Banbury'. Knightley 'matriculated at Oxford in 1685, studied law at the Inner Temple [in London], and was admitted to the Bar in 1696'. Alicia was buried in Holywell Parish in July 1725; her husband died in Northamptonshire in 1740. (All preceding quotations are from Greer et al., p. 376.)

A Poem Upon His Sacred Majesty, His Voyage for Holland … (1691)

This poem, licensed on 23 December 1690, responds to William III's decision to visit his native Holland to negotiate with fellow Protestants about their conflict with Catholic France. William had become king after the 1688 'Glorious Revolution' deposed James II, a Catholic. Although James's Protestant daughter, Mary II, theoretically ruled jointly with William (her husband), in fact she willingly subordinated herself, becoming more active only during William's frequent trips abroad. These were often resented by many of the English, but William, impatient with English political wrangling, enjoyed his trips home. He sometimes even hinted that he might abdicate and return to Holland. D'Anvers' poem, then, reflects real anxieties as well as solid support for the Protestant king.

As the poem opens, Britannia laments William's departure (p. 3). She fears that this born conqueror will lose interest in her since she is now at peace (p. 4). When Belgia solicitously asks why Britannia grieves, the latter blames Belgia, since William's visit there might tempt France to attack England (p. 4). The motherly Belgia, noting that she willingly gave William to Britain (p. 4), upbraids Britannia for lamenting his temporary absence (p. 5). Besides, she says, William returns not to make war but to plan peace. Britannia now interrupts, calling Belgia an unkind 'Step-Mother' who steals her joy, and she warns that Belgia's apparent willingness to sacrifice Britain to France will only endanger Belgia herself (pp. 5–6).

Belgia surprises Britannia by mocking the latter's effeminate degeneracy and by insisting on her own hatred for France and maternal love of William (p. 7). Although she worries that he may now share Britannia's contempt for her, she takes heart in his approach (p. 8). She alludes to his recent victories in Ireland and notes that he has left Mary behind to show his love of England (p. 8). Britannia now brightens, although she ironically condemns Belgia for not having sooner mentioned Mary's calming presence. Belgia is given the last (somewhat abrupt) reconciling words (p. 8). Greer et al. call the poem 'dull' but note that its dedication to Mary implies D'Anvers' social and poetic standing (p. 376; see also Ezell, p. 97).

The copy reproduced here, from the Houghton Library at Harvard University (shelfmark *fEC65.D2367.691p), contains the following note: 'Narcissus Luttrell's copy, priced & dated in his autograph: 2d. [&] 2. Januar'.

***Academia: or, the Humours of the University of Oxford in Burlesque Verse* (1691)**

This poem, D'Anvers's best, was apparently for sale by March 1691. It reflects detailed knowledge of Oxford and is written in 'robust colloquial iambic tetrameters, called hudibrastics. The form, popularised by Samuel Butler's *Hudibras* (1663–1678), is characterised by comic feminine rhymes and the use of slang and dialect words in contriving them' (Greer et al., p. 377). The poem is often difficult to follow, not only because of its slang and contemporary allusions but because of its frequent narrative shifts. The following summary attempts to make some sense of these.

The invocation 'To the UNIVERSITY' mixes seemingly sincere respect for Oxford with mockery of some residents who do anything but study (sig. A1r). D'Anvers explains that she satirises some of the University's '*younger sort*' merely to amuse others and please herself (sig. A2v). The poem itself explains how the muses, once respected, are now abused by negligent scholars (pp. 1–2). Although D'Anvers does not want to be 'seen to bellow, / Like a '*Girl* forsaken by a *Fellow*' (p. 2), in fact her language often seems just as rough and coarse as that of the men she mocks.

D'Anvers now describes a typical youth and his male companion who enter the university (pp. 3–4). The youth is an unsophisticated country boy monitored by an attentive '*Carrier*' instructed (and perhaps paid) by the boy's mother (p. 4). Although initially respectful and modest (pp. 4–5), the youth is soon laughed out of this politeness and now acts rudely towards everyone except his collegiate superiors. His doting mother and aunts have provided money to supply his needs, if only because they hope he will someday be a bishop (pp. 5–6). Meanwhile, the boy himself is glad to have escaped the harsh discipline of his hometown schoolmaster. He soon befriends 'Rake-Hells' who relieve him of his cash (p. 6), but just at this point of financial desperation D'Anvers interrupts to provide an amusingly long 'digression'.

She begins by noting that the sort of youth just described is not from a privileged background; he is not the kind who might eventually study law at London's Inns of Court. Rather, he is a poor scholar who might function either as a 'Servitor' (a kind of butler to wealthier students) or a 'Commoner' (the next highest rank [p. 7]). 'Gentleman Commoners' were a step further up, and D'Anvers describes the concern they sometimes received from protective mothers (p. 8). Pampered and well-fed at home, such youths (D'Anvers suggests) not only found it hard to cope with their slim college rations but also often over-ate and over-slept (pp. 8–10).

Suddenly D'Anvers digresses again – this time discussing the intimidating Latinate language Oxonians favored. Such verbiage, she implies, would puzzle even Satan, and it is certainly enough to goad the typical undergraduate (whom she nicknames '*Soph*') into earnest prayer (pp. 10–11). She describes the frustrations tutors faced when trying to instruct born fools in linguistic intricacies (p. 11), and she even suggests that such ignorance, although innate in the upper classes, may also have been exacerbated by over-eating (pp. 11–12). She claims that parents are rarely disturbed by ignorance (pp. 11–12), and she describes how Soph's father seems less interested in his son's studies than in his success at whoring and drinking (p. 12).

D'Anvers now shifts to Soph's servant, John Blunder (p. 25), who first timidly and then boastfully tells the boy's proud father how he helped encourage Soph's taste for alcohol (p. 13). John speaks in a comic country dialect (routinely using 'hoa' for 'he'), and D'Anvers must have enjoyed this character, since she now turns much of the poem over to John's bawdy narrative (addressed to fellow servants) of his Oxford adventures. His phrasing can be both amusingly gross (as when he describes how ale shot out both at their '*Noses*' and their '*Hoases*' [p. 15]) and historically exact (as when he mentions a famous drinking horn at Queen's College [p. 15]). John's own encounter with the horn left him covered in beer and vomit, especially since the '*Scollards*' had mischievously spiked the former with salt (p. 16).

John next describes the sights (and sites) of the campus and city, including a garden containing not only a giant whale bone but also trees cut to resemble a huge clown and a perching crane (pp. 16–18). John's language is entertainingly crude and also comically naive as he explains the functions of various Oxford schools (p. 19). Particularly interesting is his account of the Bodleian Library, with its over-flowing books and two great globes – one mapping the heavens, the other the earth (pp. 20–21). When noise from his nailed shoes disturbs some readers, John quickly takes them off and announces his intent to stay for the sermon, thinking the library a church (pp. 22–23). When he is laughed at, though, he leaves, coming next to the

Sheldonian Theatre (pp. 23–24), at that time home to the university press. Friendly printers (for a fee) set his name in type and commemorate the precise period of his visit – June 1682 (pp. 25–27). He describes the Theatre's painted ceiling (pp. 27–28), especially its paintings of 'the Triumph of Religion and Learning over Envy, Hatred and Malice' (see Mason, p. 72). Then he moves next door to the 'Laboratory' (now the Old Ashmolean), but the high entrance fee dissuades him from entering (p. 29).

Next morning (Sunday), John decides to visit Christ Church Cathedral (the college chapel) to hear its organ (pp. 29–30). On his way, he observes the two small mechanical 'quarter-boys' built into the tower of St. Mary's Church at Carfax, Oxford's traditional central point. These statuettes (which John thinks are living 'Pigmys') strike bells to mark each quarter-hour (pp. 30–31). By the time he takes in other Oxford landmarks, the day is over and he must postpone hearing the organ (p. 31). When he does visit the Cathedral, his description of the dress and conduct of the choristers may have been intended by D'Anvers to mock Catholic elements of Anglican worship (p. 32). Nearby the Cathedral stands Tom Tower, with its huge 6 1/4 ton bell, 'Great Tom' (p. 33; see Mason, p. 54). Other sights include the gate of Brasenose College, named after a brass-nosed knocker stolen from the original Hall in 1333 (p. 33; see Mason, p. 75), and a grotesque stone carving known as 'the Devil' of Lincoln College (p. 33).

John now turns to describing the scholars (p. 34). He mentions the square hats (resembling platters) worn by some and the looser caps worn by others; the latter remind him of an old woman's toothless mouth (p. 34). He describes the fashion for well-worn, tattered gowns, since such garments implied seniority (pp. 34), and he mistakenly assumes that the gowns prescribed for the lowest-ranking students are sleeveless because their hungry owners have been forced to sell the cloth to buy food (pp. 34–35; see Midgley, pp. 13–14). Finally, he notes other gowns so wide that they seem to be held out as if for drying – a comment that leads a fellow servant, Tom, to assume that that they must have been pissed in (pp. 35–36). On this farcical note, John's story ends and the original tale resumes where it had broken off – with its focus on the entering student and his friend (p. 37).

The two freshmen are now enamored (respectively) of alcohol and women (p. 37); both are so devoted to eating and drinking that they literally polish the tables with their elbows (pp. 37–38). Such habits inevitably lead to lack of '*Ready*' money (pp. 38–39), making it necessary to '*run a Tick*' (i.e., buy on credit [p. 39]). Students then must often hide from creditors (p. 40). When money arrives from home, some scholars head off to nearby Headington to spend it on a 'mistress' – apparently an experienced prostitute of the sort who sets traps ('*Gins*') for fools (pp. 40–41). Other students court local girls but satirise them in verse if they resist, much as the 'Terrae Filius', a kind of licensed satirist, mocked members of the University and community at the yearly graduation gathering known as the 'Act' (pp. 42–43). During this ceremony, graduates submitted to public oral examinations, although some apparently stationed friends in the hall to signal correct answers through silent hand gestures (pp. 43–44).

Students, after all, can't be expected to study when there is so much else to do. Thus on Sundays they move from church to church (often scouting women), scurrying as quickly as if they suffered from diarrhoea (pp. 44–45). One scholar is even annoyed when a Quaker angrily objects to his kissing the Quaker's wife during a service; after all, the woman herself doesn't seem to mind! (pp. 45–47). The husband reports the incident to a University proctor (or disciplinary officer), but the only punishment is a required essay (either largely plagiarised or stale and hackneyed), its Latin as rough as coarse linen compared to satin (pp. 47–48). Although scholars are theoretically expected to study, visits by friends and family or trips to London provide only two of many possible distractions (pp. 48–50).

When Soph forgets to buy tobacco before the college closes at 9 p.m., he instead smokes straw from his mattress. And, although he usually misses obligatory morning prayers, he makes sure he is up early for lessons from a famous dancing-master (pp. 50–51). Those who rise too soon risk encountering chilly, foggy weather, but the more experienced learn to avoid such hindrances (p. 51). Meanwhile, scholars who hunt often descend on poor but welcoming country-folk to scrounge free meals, although sometimes another of their goals (or '*Butts*') is the surreptititous theft of a hunk (or 'flitching') of bacon or a tempting chicken (pp. 52–53). Similarly, after drinking at nearby taverns, they often go outside, pretending to relieve themselves but then dashing off without paying, and stealing tavern property in the process (pp. 53–54).

Next morning, the tavern hostess and other bill collectors storm the thieves' rooms, but the guilty students stay locked inside (pp. 54–55). Evasive maneuvers eventually help them escape their cheated (or '*bubbl'd*') creditors (pp. 55–58). The latter, however, apparently over-charge sufficiently to afford losses; their dunning is motivated mainly by greed (pp. 58–59). To avoid them, indebted scholars often take comically convoluted detours (pp. 60–62).

Next day, the creditors once more crowd outside the elusive student's door (pp. 62–63). Their exasperated number even includes the mother of Soph's (or 'Mr. Snear's') illegitimate child (pp. 63-66). So persistent are they that Snear eventually decides to quit Oxford. That night, while leaving, he beats an inquiring proctor, smashes a few windows, and filches some property, content with knowing that he can always study law in London (p. 66). The poem now comes full circle: it began by describing Soph's arrival and ends by describing Snear's departure – a departure mourned as much by his creditors as by the mother(s) of his abandoned illegitimate children (p. 67).

The copy of *Academia* reproduced here, from the Folger Shakespeare Library (shelfmark 140441q), was once owned by Francis Edwards; a catalogue note reads as follows: 'Disbound; remnants of binding on spine. Sewing holes stabbed through text block near spine'.

The Oxford-Act: A Poem (1693)

Although this poem was published anonymously in 1693, a contemporary note attributes it to D'Anvers; certainly it resembles *Academia*, and most subsequent scholars assume it is hers. Smith and Cardinale question this attribution (p. 246) on the grounds that the narrator and the characters speak as males, but this fact can be reconciled with D'Anvers's authorship if the poem is seen as a dramatic farce rather than as autobiograpical journalism. The poem focuses on the annual (if intermittent) university 'Act', part of a larger 'encaenia' or commencement ceremony which lasted for several days and included many rituals. These included comically satirical 'Musick speeches' and a licensed but often bawdy diatribe by the 'Terrae filius' (i.e., son of the earth, or bastard). Greer et al. note that D'Anvers's own father had performed this role in 1657 (p. 378).

The poem's narrator, apparently from Cambridge, announces plans to observe the famous Oxford 'Act' – a ceremony discontinued for so long that many assume it never existed (pp. 1–2). Even the most learned cannot now say when the Act, featuring 'Terrae-Filius', was last conducted. Apparently its demise followed the Duke of Monmouth's unsuccessful Protestant rebellion, in 1685, against James II – a rebellion that mostly Tory Oxford had opposed (p. 2). Nevertheless, the narrator sarcastically notes the subsequent 'gratitude' of James, whose relations with Oxford ironically soured following Monmouth's defeat. In dealing with both Monmouth and Oxford, James relied heavily on Chief Justice George Jeffreys, to whom the narrator attributes the temporary cessation of the Act. The ceremony was revived only after the 1688 'Glorious Revolution' (pp. 2–3).

The narrator next describes the motley crowd travelling to Oxford (pp. 3–4). This includes two booksellers and an author, who discuss (among other matters) the latest victims of some London wits and satirists known as the Athenians (p. 4). Talk then turns to an earlier agreement by which the booksellers and author would mutually profit from a new writing project. They decide to focus on the Act itself, and, once the travelling author is assured he will not be cheated, he agrees to the deal (pp. 6–7). He promises that if the booksellers will help spy on the Act, he will poetically record their gossip (p. 7).

His account begins by mentioning the participants' dress (pp. 10–11), the hierarchical seating (p. 11), the proper response to satirical speeches (p. 11), and the names of particular proctors (p. 12). Also mentioned are the technical term for the dressing-room (p. 12), the preaching of St. Antony of Egypt (p. 12), the extreme youth of some students (p. 12), the purchased satires performed by many older scholars unwilling to acknowledge their ghost-writers (p. 13). Subjects of the purchased poems include the riches of the Bodleian, recent British victories over France, an earthquake in Italy, the military prowess of the second Duke of Ormonde, conflict between France and the Savoy, the illness of that duchy's prince, and the consternation his illness caused among other members of the Grand Alliance (p. 13).

The poem then mentions a degree candidate named Budgell whose speech attacked both the Pope and the Protestant followers of Lelio Sozini (Socinus); another speaker named Tod who discussed religious conflicts, particularly one concerning the divinity of Christ (a view associated with St. Athanasius); still another speaker (from Brasenose College) who attacked both the Calvinism of Geneva and the Socinianism associated with Cracow; another speaker's opinions on deism; and various other matters (p. 14). Canto II ends with a report on how speakers and audience alike subsequently relax at a tennis court (pp. 14–15).

Canto III opens by alluding to an aggressive character from Dryden's *Conquest of Granada* who resembles the 'Terrae Filius'. Using a Greek term, the poet fancifully implies that the latter figure springs from the earth (p. 15), almost like a humming insect that aims for the sky (p. 16). These remarks lead to discussion of various mythic earth-born rebels, who are figuratively the progenitors of such human satirists as the writers of ancient Greek 'Old Comedy', including Aristophanes, who famously lampooned Socrates and (allegedly) even the philosopher's wife, Xantippe (p. 16). In describing how such satire migrated to England, the poem mentions alternative names for Oxford and cites the writings of Anthony a Wood, the famous (if reclusive) university historian, whose work is said to surpass writings of other chroniclers such as Peter Heylyn and John Harmar (p. 17). The narrator concedes, however, that the 'Terrae Filius' may be related to similar figures in old Cornish 'miracle' plays who sprang out of holes (unlike the Greek *deus ex machina*, who was lowered onto the stage [p. 17]). Perhaps, the narrator says, such satire moved from Oxford to Cornwall rather than vice versa. He also discusses the origins of the 'music speech', wondering whether it perhaps derived from performances of various street musicians (p. 17).

The poem notes that despite the sting of the 'Terrae Filius'' metaphorical whip, such satire is popular. Particular topics and targets are cited (p. 18), and the speech and traits of one speaker – a linguist named Smith – are detailed at length (pp. 19–20). Smith's speech teases the ladies present. He claims that although he is no physician, he is eager to provide gynecological help, and he mocks other men with similar inclinations (pp. 20–21). He claims his speech has not been plagiarised, and he ends abruptly after describing how one lady rejected him in favor of an uglier rival (p. 22). D'Anvers's poem itself also ends abruptly after the narrator comments on women's fickle tastes and also on how men and women, like teasing male and female cats, often feud before eventually making love.

The copy of *The Oxford-Act* reproduced here is from The Huntington Library (shelfmark 105674).

References

Wing D221 [*Poem Upon His Sacred Majesty*]; Wing D220 [*Academia*]; Wing O847 [*Oxford-Act*]
Ezell, Margaret J.M. (1987), *The Patriarch's Wife: Literary Evidence and the History of the Family*, Chapel Hill, NC: University of North Carolina Press
Greer, Germaine et al. (eds.), (1989), *Kissing the Rod: An Anthology of Seventeenth-Century Women's Verse*, New York: Noonday Press
Mason, Mercia (1987), *Blue Guide: Oxford and Cambridge*, New York: Norton
Midgley, Graham (1996), *University Life in Eighteenth-Century Oxford*, New Haven: Yale University Press
Smith, Hilda L., and Susan Cardinale (1990), *Women and the Literature of the Seventeenth Century*, New York: Greenwood
Stevenson, Jane and Peter Davidson (eds), (2001), *Early Modern Women Poets (1520–1700): An Anthology*, Oxford: Oxford University Press
Tyacke, Nicholas, (ed.), (1997), *The History of the University of Oxford*, vol. 4, *Seventeenth-Century Oxford*, Oxford: Clarendon Press

ROBERT C. EVANS

Acknowledgements

Many thanks to the reference and photographic staffs at the Folger, Houghton, and Huntington libraries, and especially to the unflappable Georgianna Ziegler and Michael Scott of the Folger. Travel to all three libraries was supported by a research grant from Auburn University, Montgomery. For their patience, guidance and 'close readings', sincere thanks are also due to Patrick Cullen, Anne Lake Prescott, and Betty Travitsky.

A Poem upon His Sacred Majesty ... (Wing D221) is reproduced, by permission, from the copy in the Houghton Library at Harvard University (shelfmark *fEC65.D2367.691p). Text block of the title page is 246 mm × 148 mm. The text-block of inside pages measures 255 mm × 140 mm.

2ᵈ

A

POEM

UPON

His Sacred Majesty,

𝕳𝖎𝖘 𝖁𝖔𝖞𝖆𝖌𝖊 𝖋𝖔𝖗 𝕳𝖔𝖑𝖑𝖆𝖓𝖉:

By way of

DIALOGUE,

BETWEEN

Belgia and Britannia.

By Mʳˢ· *D'ANVERS.*

L'ICENS'D,

December 23.
1690.

J. F.

LONDON,
Printed for *Tho. Bever,* at the *Hand* and *Star,* near
Temple Barr, in *Fleet-street,* MDCXCI. 2.*Januar:*

TO THE
High and Mighty PRINCESS
MARY
𝕼𝖚𝖊𝖊𝖓 𝖔𝖋 𝕲𝖗𝖊𝖆𝖙 𝕭𝖗𝖎𝖙𝖆𝖎𝖓, &c.

ALICIA D'ANVERS
Humbly Dedicates this POEM.

BRITANNIA.

WRetched *Britannia*! Haplefs, and undone!
   How have my Follies call'd this Vengeance down,
   And anger d Heav'n to fo fevere a Frown ?
Shall a Curft Nicety of Honours Law,
Tug from thefe Fondling Arms, my Dear *Naffaw* ?
Councils, or hated bufinefs, call thee hence !
To Love, and Me, nothing's a juft pretence.
Injurious War! Curfe on the very Word ;
Unkind *Bellona*, if thou ft call'd my Lord,
Shield that dear Bofom from the Ungentle Sword.

Gods !

Gods!——Should *Britannia* find that Rival there;
What ill remains? What is there left to fear?
Had not rough Sounds, and Groans of Dying Foes,
Charm'd thy brave Youth, I had ignor'd thefe Woes.
Now lefs belov'd, and fewer Charms I wear
Than Wounds, or Death it felf receiv'd in War;
Ah me! Why was he born a Conquerour?

BELGIA.

What Dæmon fills thy boding Soul with Fears
Nymph, What has rais'd this Storm of Sighs and Tears

BRITANNIA

Can you demand? 'Tis a Difcourteous part;
To give the Wound, and wonder at the Smart.
Have you not rent my Heart, and ftab'd my Soul,
And all my Joys with my dear *Albion* ftole?
By you at once of Love, and Guard bereft,
And to the Triumphs of Proud *Gallia* left.
Cruel——yet to fuch Griefs you'd add Reftraint,
And check the Ecchoes of my loud Complaint.

BELGIA.

Thou Rav'ft, Fond Maid, fuch Idle Dreams as thefe
Affift thy Impatience to o'erthrow thy Peace:
Gave I not firft thy *Albion* to thy Arms,
Bold, and Undaunted, full of Martial Charms?
In Armour were his firft Approaches made,
And Warlike Sounds the only Serenade:
Your Infant Loves by War more Sinewy grew,
While *Mars* on *Albion* fmil'd, no lefs than you.
Here could I tell the Everlafting Story,
Of my *Naffaw*, and Noble *Albion*'s Glory.

Had

Had not the dazling luftre of his Name,
Already fill'd the wondering World with Fame.
To you, 'twere but Impertinence to prove
The fole Inducement of the Heart to Love
Can you forget what Charms in Honour dwells?
Honour, Divineft of all Magick Spells
By which my Daftard Soul's fecur'd from fear,
And the hoarfe Sounds of War delight my Ear.
Suppofe our lov'd *Naffaw*, by fierce Alarms,
(The Voice of Glory) fummon'd to his Arms.
My Tears were an unpardonable Wrong,
What General e'er was harm'd who Honour won?
Muft fuch fond Sorrows injure *Albion* ?
Have I lefs Love than you? Is he lefs mine?
Yet I can hold a Grief like yours a Crime;
I'd fcorn to own, nay Blufh, to think a Sin,
You've indulg'd your Heart fo fondly in,
Methinks you're bold indeed, who dare Repine
At the Commiffion of the Powers Divine;
Since they are pleas'd to honour *Albion* fo,
While Heaven directs as Generaliffimo,
But e'er I pufh thefe Martial Thoughts too far,
Which I perceive fo ungrateful to their Ear.
Leaft your mad Paffion by miftake be fain'd,
Know I've not call'd your *Albion* to Command,
But to Confult, and to fecure your eafe,
His bufinefs!——*Belgia* and *Britannia*'s Peace——
And can his Abfence, fuch well manag'd Hours,
Admit of fuch Ungrateful Sighs as yours?
Blufh at the foolifh Fondnefs of a Bride——

BRITANNIA.

Blufh at the wild Excurfions of your Pride.
My *Albion* ! Could my *Albion* come from you,
Be my kind Lord, and not ungentle too.

B   Well,

Well, my Step-Mother, now too late I've feen,
What all Your Actions, and Your Drifts have been.
Why were my Praifes fpoke to *Albion*;
Call'd Fair, and Lov'd, and Courted, and Undone?
Malicious *Gallia* could but Curfe my Joys
Which *Belgia* gave, and fhe alone deftroys
Now the Fantaftick Ape, Laughs, fhews her Teeth,
While the dull Croud refounds my killing Grief;
But fince my Tears muft buy you *Gallia's* Smile,
No more let me be. call'd the Happy Ifle:
My Tears——Alas! your Cruelties are more,
*Y*ou'd quench her thirfty Vengeanee with my Gore
No fooner fhall my dear *Naffaw* be gone;
Neatly retir'd, by yuor Pretences home,
But *Gallia* claps her Ponyard in my fide,
And clears the way for a more Beauteous Bride.
Fonder——More Foolifh *Belgia*, to fuppofe
That my Remove fhall not increafe your Foes.
Mine fhall defpife thee, for the Inhuman Deed,
But for thy Crimes, Why fhould my *Albion* bleed?
For whom you fpread your Machavillian Snares,
And fill with dull (to me dull) State Affairs.
Frown not, my *Albion*, though I difapprove,
The kindnefs of my dear miftaken Love,
I fhake not for my worthlefs felf fo much,
As I can die to think thy dangers fuch.
Can *Belgia* boaft in thee a larger fhare?
She may——but not her Love with mine compare,
Should *Albion* fall her Honour's Sacrifice,
Could her harfh Voice adorn his Obfequies,
Like the foft Mournings of my tender Crys

BELGIA.

Then my harfh Voice offends your Curious Ear.
In your fair Eyes, I'm Ridicul'd, I fear,

But

But fince you've been pleas'd to affront me
No fears of mine forbid to let you know
That you *Britannia* have been found of late,
Soft to a Scorn, Nice and Effeminate
Prom your Brave Anceftors degenerate.

BRITANNIA

Hold Angry Matron, hold, What have I done
Pardon the hafty Errors of my Tongue,

BELGIA

'Tis your Erroneous Zeal for *Albion*,
Which, I believe has offer'd me the wrong,
But your blind Love for him fhall ever be
Pretence, thus to reproach, and injure me
Britannia, the juft Gods, as well as their,
Could ne'er forget fo black a Perjury,
Wou'd I pleafe *Gallia* with thy Overthrow,
Could Hell contrive and break fo ftrict a Vow
You hear'd when I againft the Strumpet fwore,
Then let her Name offend my Ear no more.
Nor is this all, you'r bolder yet, and dare
Cenfure the Love I to your *Albion* bear,
You're Young, and Smooth, and fcorn thefe rough old Hands;
Which wrapt his tender Sides in Swadling Bands;
T i strue, proud Nymph, what you difdain to own,
Thefe Wither'd Breafts gave Suck to *Albion*.
While on my Careful Knee Heaven's Darling fate,
By this Knee rais'd to a more Glorious Fate.
The Child with Lawrels play'd, and fmil'd on Bays,
While in his Ear I fung his future praife.
This hoarfe rough Voice, which you fo much defpife,
Oft brought kind *Morpheus* to his half-clos'd Eyes,
Shall not a Nurfe, and Tender Mother too,
Feel Pangs of Love as fharp, and ftrong as you.

B   Shall

Shall Nuptial Vows, or Fair *Britannia*'s Charms
For ever lock my *Albion* in her Arms ?
Lock him for ever from these Longing Eyes,
Belgia (ye Gods !) with Expectation dies.
Why have I Wish'd, and Sigh'd so long in vain ?
Partakes *Nassaw* of his soft Brides Disdain,
And fears to see his Wrinkled Face again ?
He has gaz'd upon thy Winning Face so long
'Till I'm scorn'd as much by *Albion* —
But see he comes, spight of thy Wrath he'll come.
Nassaw, now to the Gods I'll trust again,
Those Gods I never trusted yet in vain ;
When poor *Hibernia* call'd him to her aid,
(Whose gashly Wounds, made *Mars* himself afraid)
'Twas those kind Gods return'd the Mortal Blow,
Heaven will not spare him yet——I *Belgia* know
There's greater things for *Albion* yet to do
But hold——*Britannia*, you've forgot, I find,
How dear a Pledge your Lord has left behind ; ——
Thou Smil'st again, How fast thy Sorrow dies,
Sorrow, the Fair *Britannia*'s worst Disguise !
Fresh Beauties in thy Cheeks themselves display !
What can the Lovely change pretend to say ?

B R I T A N N I A.

That I no more can for his Absence mourn,
Who leaves so dear a Pledge of his Return,
Belgia 'twas cruel, and your fault indeed,
To let my Soul so long with Sorrows bleed,
You've wrong'd my Heart, (*Belg.*) Then there was wrong for
Give me your hand, be Friends, and I'll a'done.   (wrong,

F I N I S.

16

ACADEMIA:

OR, THE

HUMOURS

OF THE

Univerſity of Oxford.

IN

BURLESQUE Verſe.

By Mrs. *Alicia D'Anvers.*

LONDON,

Printed and ſold by *Randal Taylor* near *Stationers*
Hall. 1691.

TO THE

UNIVERSITY

Ail peaceful Shade, whose sacred verdant side
Bold Thamisis salutes, hail Noble Tide ;
Hail Learning's Mother, hail Great Brittains Pride.
Hail to thy lovely Groves, and Bowers, wherein
Thy Hea'ven begotten Darlings sit, and sing ;
Thy First-born Sons, who shall in After-Story
Share thy loud Fame, as now they bring thee Glory.

Arriv'd at such a rich Maturity,
Those who spell Man so well, would blush to be
Took at the Mothers Breast, or Nurses Knee;
Much more in filth to wallow Shoulder high,
In Tears, till his kind Nurse had laid him dry.

A   Actions

To the UNIVERSITY.

Actions that give no blush of Guilt, or Shame,
To those so young, that yet they want a Name,
(I've heard that Brute, and Infant are the same.)
Then beauteous Matron, frown not on me for't.
Tho at the triflings of your younger sort,
I smile so much; since all I hope to do,
Is but to raise your Smiles, and others too,
And please my self, if pardon'd first by you.

ACADEMIA

ACADEMIA

OR THE

HUMOURS

OF THE

𝔘𝔫𝔦𝔳𝔢𝔯𝔰𝔦𝔱𝔶 𝔬𝔣 𝔒𝔵𝔣𝔬𝔯𝔡.

I'Intend to give you a *Relation*,
As prime as any is in the *Nation*:
The Name of th' place is--- let me see,
Call'd moſt an end the *'Verſity*;
In which ſame place, as Story tells,
Liv'd once *Nine* handſome bonny *Girls*,
Highly in *olden Time* reputed,
Tho' now ſo thwačťd and perſecuted;

B   *Schollars*

Schollars belike now can't abide 'um,
So that they're fain to fcout and hide 'um,
Or's fure as you're alive they'd beat 'um ;
Out of the place they'd *chofe to feat 'um,*
And they who won't be feen to maul 'um,
Revile, befpatter 'um, or becall 'um.
E'ne thefe fly *Curs* would *Strumpets* make 'um,
When e're they catch 'um can, or take um,
And pinch 'um, till they've made 'um fing ye,
The filthy'ft ftuff as one can bring ye;
The end of all fuch *Rafcals* wooing,
Proves many 'a heedlefs *Girle's* undoing :
All thefe, and twenty more *Abufes,*
Are daily offer'd to the *Mufes.*
You may perceive, I'me mightily
Difturb'd, they're us'd fo fpitefully ;
And muft confefs, where's no denying,
That I can hardly hold from crying;
But that I mayn't be feen to bellow,
Like 'Girl forfaken by a *Fellow,*
Roar, throw my Snot about, and blubber,
Like *School-Boys,* or an am'rous *Lubber,*

I'ld

I'le lay aſide my *Bowels* yearning,
And talk of *Schollars,* and their *Learning.*

When the young *Farmer,* or young *Farrier,*
Comes jogging up with's *Country Carrier,*
Well hors'd as he, for I have ſeen 'um
Both have but one good *Horſe* between 'um :
But two *Bums,* with one *Horſe* there under,
Is no great matter of a wonder ;
For ſome are fain to ride o'th 'packing,
Made eaſie with good *Straw,* and *Sacking,*
Kindly contriv'd for's *Buttocks* ſake,
Which otherwiſe might chance to ake :
But then there's no great fear of tumbling,
Altho the *Nag* were giv'n to ſtumbling ;
He can't be hurt (Sir,) if you'd have him,
Say he ſhou'd fall, the pack would ſave him :
So that if I might tell my mind, Sir,
I'd's live ride ſo, as ride behind Sir.
Then if the *Young-Mans Band* or *Cravit,*
Handkerchief, Neck-cloath, what you'll have it,

Be ill put on, or off be blow'n,
The *Carrier* tyes, or pins it on;
Or he had been a very *Clown*, to
Be bred and born i'th same *Town* too.
And knew his Friends so well, and knew him,
That wou'dn't have been civil to him;
Beside, a charge given by his *Mother*,
To use him kinder than another.

Now being arrived at his *Colledge*,
The place of *Learning*, and of *Knowledge*;
A while he'll leer about, and snivel ye,
And doff his Hat to all most civilly,
Being told at home that a shame Face too,
Was a great sign he had some *Grace* too,
He'l speak to none, alas! for he's
Amaz'd at every Man he sees :
May-hap this lasts a *Week*, or two,
Till some *Scab* laughs him out on't, so,
That when most you'd expect his mending,
His Breeding,s ended, and not ending :

Now he dares walk abroad, and dare ye,
Hat on, in Peoples *Faces* stare ye,
Thinks what a *Fool* he was before, to
Pull off his Hat, which he'd no more do;
But that the *Devil* shites *Disasters*,
So that he's forc'd to cap the *Masters*,
He might have nail'd it to his *Head*, else,
And wore it *Night*, and *Day* a *Bed*, else,
And then de'e see, for I'de have you mind it,
He had always known where to find it;
But of a bad thing, make the best say,
And of two Evils chuse the least pray,
He must cap them; but for all other,
Tho 'twere his Father, or his Mother,
His Gran'um, Unckle, Aunt, or Cousin,
He wo' not give one Cap to a dozen;
Tho you must know he flows with Mony,
Giv'n by his Mam, unto her Hony;
His Aunts, their Six-pence were apiece too,
Having had the luck to sell their Geese to
Some profit, that same Market-day,
Being th' o're night he came away:

But

But f'rall they were so loving to him,
Besure they'd always see him doing,
Because they entertained this Hope,
In time he might become a Bishop ;
That often he had cause to grumble,
Under thick-fisted Master Fumble :
The Master of the School was he,
And flash'd him for his good, de'e see,
Beating his Brains into his Collar,
That he might prove the better Schollar.
He looks upon it as a Blessing
Beyond his wish and his expressing ;
A good Substantial, and no Fiction,
To be free from his Jurisdiction,
With's Fellow Rake-Hells gets acquainted,
Who might i'th Country have been Sainted.
These kindly hug young Soph, and squeeze him,
And of his Cash t' a Farthing ease him ;
This being done, and being so,
He's at a loss now what to do.
So here I'le leave him, I must tell ye,
With a Heart panting in his Belly ;

But

But left Defpair prove his undoing,
E're long I'le come again unto him,
With fome of's hackle and profeffion,
Tho I muft make a fhort digreffion;
Thefe being of another fort, then
Thofe who're defign'd for Inns of Court-men.
Who moft an end come up a Horfe-back,
Tho many a time they're *brought* a *pick-pack*,
Like Geefe to Market, niddle, noddle,
So high, no mar'l their Brains prove oddle.
Another fort of idle Loaches
Come lolling up to Town in Coaches;
Thofe I've fpoken of, de'e obferve me,
Either's a Servitor to ferve ye,
Brings Bread and Beer, or what is call'd for,
Eating what's left, Trencher and all (Sir:)
Or elfe a Commoner may be,
And thinks himfelf better than he,
Becaufe he fhou'd pay for his eating,
But can't, unlefs you'l take a beating.
The next, who 'as leave to domineer,
Adds Gentleman to Commoner,

Moft

Most dearly tender'd by his Mother,
Who loves him better than his Brother;
So she at home, a good while keeps him,
In White-broath, and Canary steeps him:
And tho his Noddle's somewhat empty,
His Guts are stuft with Sweet-meats plenty;
Madam's most sadly tosticated,
Knowing her Boy but empty-pated,
Lest the soft *Squire might starved be*,
When e're he's sent to 'th' *Verfity*; ·
Which to prevent, and to befriend him,
A Pye, or Cake, she'll quickly send him,
Directed for her loving Son,
Living i'th Colledge in Oxford Town;
Charging her Man to let him know,
That they're all well, and hope he's so:
But what his Mother sent up with him,
Being much more than now she gives him,
And all consum'd; he thinks it best
To hide, and eat by himself the rest:
His will at home (Sir,) always having,
But made his Stomach, the more craving;

May-

May hap they'd twenty hundred *Dishes*,
And twenty thousand fort of *Fishes*,
Of which, when but a little Elf,
He'd eat the greatest part himself;
De'e think then 'twould not make the *young Lad*
At a *Three half pence* Meat become *sad*,
Which at the *Colledge*, you muft know, Man's
No more, nor lefs; than one *Boys* Commons?
And then, they make a hideous clutter
For a *Farth'n Drink*, *Bread*, *Cheefe*, or *Butter*;
And would that pay, now, in your thinking,
For wafhing of the *Pot* they drink in?
Yet for all this, his *Tutor* cryes ye,
Sufficient 'tis, and may fuffice ye;
Knowing from being *bred a Schollar*,
Much *eating* breeds both *Flegm*, and *Coller*,
Much *praying* him, does much advife it,
If he loves *Learning*, to defpife it:
Glutt'ony (thinks *Soph*,) who e're abhorr'd it,
That had wherewith, and could afford it?
Tho' like a *Log* he ftands, he's thinking,
He lives by *eating*, and by *drinking*,

C

And

And finds it fo unreafonable,
He mayn't *eat* all that comes to Table;
That truth, he may advife him to't,
But for his part he'll never do't,
Preach till his *heart akes*, of forbearing,
He for his fhare, will ne're be fparing ;
And when he's told *'tis naught for's head*, to
Lye all the livelong *day* a-bed fo ;
He fears his *Tutor* would prevent
His having any *Nourifhment*.

    When *Categorematical*,
A Word, you'd think the *Devil* and all,
But hold! --- I think there is another,
Should a' took place as *Elder Brother*,
'Tis, let me fee, now, whach'ee call,
Syncategorematical.
Were it *Old Nick*, enough to mufle him,
For all his years, and ftanding, puzle him;
Soph, when this comes, (as I was faying,)
Begins to know the ufe of *praying*,

                              Blefling

Blessing *himself*, and his *Relations*,
From these, and such like *Conjurations* ;
Master Existence, almost mad is,
To see one *stupid* as this *Lad* is,
And *'faith* and *troth*, it is a woe thing,
When he need say no more then, *nothing*
You mean by those long words, or *something* ;
Then en't the *Logger head* a *Bumpkin* :
For's pains the *Tutor* but a *looby*,
To make this *hubbub* with a *Booby* ;
And think, that all his care can do,
May alter, what he's *born* unto :
A *Fool* both *bred*, and *born* was he,
Was so *begot*, and so *must be* ;
And's *Mother'd* have him so, the rather
That in him, she might see his *Father*.
'Tis not a *Tutors* circumspection,
Can keep the *Blockhead* from *infection*,
While the *Distemper's* in his *Nature*,
You must expect him a *Man-hater* ;
Being one o'th *Puppys* o'th' *Nation*,
Both by descent, and inclination,

Follow-

Following his *Noble Anceſtors,*
A company of *lazy Curs,*
Bord'ring like them, ſo much on Beaſt,
Loves what's the fartheſt off the leaſt ;
Tho's *Tutor* thinks his *over-dulneſs*
Comes from his often *over-fulneſs,*
And that his *Brains* become ſo muddy,
From having *Paſtys* in his Study ;
But he might lay aſide that fear,
Could he but find one two days there ;
But why, not *eating* do him *good* tho',
By *breeding Brains* as well as *Blood* ſo.

No matter, tho' his *Tutor* jobes him,
His *Father* but the better loves him,
Asking, If's *Son* has got a *Punck* yet,
Whores ye, and gets ye often *drunk* yet ;
Being told by's *Man,* he took him *quaffing,*
For joy he burſts his ſides with *laughing* :
And prithee *John* (ſays he) and how was't?
Ha, *drunk 'ith'* Cellar, *as a Sow,* vvaſt?

John

John simpers, makes a *Leg*, or so ;
And since his *Worships* pleas'd to know,
An't like ye, we were something *mellow*,
For I Sir, and another Fellow----
The *justice* growing into a Passion,
Cuts him 'ith' midst of his Relation,
Cries, where was your *young Master Sirrah?*
O ho, quoth *John*---and say--- *where wor' a,*
Down in the *Cellar* too, I wot,
But I was so goun, I *de forgot,*
For I've a lamentable head,
'Specially when I'me *cut 'ith' Leg,*
But Master, (Sir) need never spare it,
Hoa has a pure *strung head* to bear it ;
And so 'ud need (Sir for ought I know,
Few *Scholards* are so learn'd as *hoa ;*
I'de give your *Worship* all my *earning,*
To have hoa's stock (Sir) of *Book-learning ;*
Something (Sir,) did my Master say,
For I was bent, to bring't away,
But I've a plaguee *Head-Piece*---look now.
I ha't--- 'twas *Latin,* for the *Cook* now,

Hoa

Hoa call'd him *Choke us*--- fo't muft be,
I knew 'twas fomewhat of *Cookery*.

Here my *Old Mafter* laughs moft furely,
Tho' *John* looks all the while demurely;
And while he's pleas'd *beyond expreffion*,
To underftand his Sons *Profeffion*;
John fteals out to the place they wifh him,
I mean, *among the Maids 'ith Kitchin*;
They'd got there too, *young Mafter's Sifter*,
Her Mother yet not having *mift her*;
They that wa'n't there, were very forry,
All longing fo to hear *John's Story*,
Of where, and how, and what hea'd feen,
And in what *Colleges* hea'd been;
Thus having made a general Mufter,
The Men and Maids got of a Clufter,
Having all bid him *welcome home*, John,
Befs fcatching of her Pate, cries, *come* John,
How does my little Mafter do?
Cries *John*, no *fmall one*, now I trow;

Now, fhould you fee'n, you wou'dn't known,
O Ceremony I hoa's *hougely* grown !
Make a brave Man, *but given grace* ;
Why, hoa lives in a fweetly place;
(Crys *Tom,*) he made you welcome furely :
O ay (cryes *John,*) we revel'd purely !
Our *Tenants* feaft to that, mun nothing's,
We purg'd, as we had dranck at both ends.
Count, what came tumbling down our *Hoafes,*
Befide what flew out from our *Nofes*;
'Twould make one fplit ones *Guts* I fwear tho,
But for my part it made me ftare tho;
There's in the *Cellar,* to my thinking,
* A *Horn,* or fomething elfe to drinck in,
Which being fill'd full, as it can hold,
'Tis his that drincks it off I'm told ;
But here's the thing that makes the rout,
When you drinck deep it flyes about,
And dout's one's *Eyes,* and makes one cough,
So that one ne're can tope it off;
Such *ugly tricks* I can't endure, I,
For't fpoil'd the Band *Sue* vvafh'd fo purely,

* At Queens there is fuch a Horn, but Johns Defcription is fufficient.

And

And all my *Bosome* fell adovvn too,
When I'de no other *Shirt* in *Town* too ;
And 'cause they'l have no *Fresh-men* there,
At first the *Scollards* salt one's bear ;
O law! I vvish'd my self at home;
It made me *spue* so ; ay (says *Tom,*)
As good a staid at home and thresh *John,*
And so have ever been a *Freshman* ;
And vvhere vvas this (cryes *Bess,*) at *Queens,*
There Mr. *William* vvent it seems,
Queens, ay (says *John,*) as neat a place
As could be made to hold her *Grace :*
O ay (cryes *Tom,*) I think I've heard so,
The *Queen* was once a *Schollar* there too ;
(Cries *John,*) 'tis true, from thence it came,
That ever since it has her *Name.*

   Tom asks, what fine things to be seen,
Beside the *Colledge* of the *Queen* ?
(Cries *John*) a many in the *Town :*
First there's a houge'ous *masty* * *Clown,*
As you go into th' *Physick Garden,*
Master ne're shew'd me, but I star'd in,

                                 The

* *A Tree cut into the shape of a Giant, the Face Alablaster.*

The *Yat's* all hung about with *whimwhoms,*
As *Fishes Bones,* and other *thingums :*
This *Giant* ſtands as you come firſt in,
For *I took heart* at laſt to thruſt in ;
His *Head* has got an *Iron Cap* on,
To keep of *Showers,* or what might happen ;
His *Face* is like a *Man's,* to ſee to,
And yet his *Bodies* but a *Tree* too :
Strutting, 'a holds a *Club* on's *Shoulder,*
Which makes him look more *fierce* and *bolder ;*
And I was told there was another,
Which now is * *dead,* and was his *Brother :*   * *There was two of theſe, the great Froſt deſtroyed one.*
I went on th' other ſide to eye'n,
Not careing much to come to nye'n ;
Leaſt with *his Club* he ſhould be doing ;
But the *Folks* ſaid, one might go to him :
But for my part, I did not care,
To look in's *Face* he did ſo ſtare.
There lyes a * *Tooth,* I tell a *Fib* too,---   * *A great Whale-bone.*
Some call't a *Tooth,* but moſt a *Rib* do.
A vaſt thing 'tis, what e're it be,
And put there for a *Rarity.*

D   When

When you are gone a little further,
You happen juft on fuch another:
* *A Crane* it is, as *People* tell ye,
Grow'ing from a *Tree Stalk* by the *Belly*.
Whether alive or no's, no knowing,
Her *Bill* touts up, juft as if *crowing*.

    Well! they all *blefs'd themfelves* that heard it,
How *John* beheld it, and here feen'd it;
But what they ftood the moft upon Sir,
Was how he flip't by the *Mad Monfter*:
Which made his *Fellow Servants* fay,
John had more mind to *Sights* then they.
But as for *Elfabeth*, fhe cry'd,
If I had feen it, I had dy'd:
John being *wifer*, term'd them *Fools*,
Well, thence I hobl'd to the *Schools*:
Liftning (cryes *John*,) to hear a *Noife* there,
But then belike there were no *Boys* there.
For if there had, there'd been a lurry,
Such as *Dogs* make, that *Cattle* worry.

Look

* A Tree cut in the fhape of a crane.

Look ye, the *Houſen* all are *Tyl'd*,
The *Door* way's *Pitch'd*; it was ſo foil'd
With the *damn'd Stones*, where one goes,
They do ſo knock, and bump ones *Toes*.
The *Schools* de'e mark's a very fair place,
With *Rooms* built round it, but a ſquare place.
The *Doors* all ſomething writ upon,
By which there's ſomething may be known.
I ask'd a *Scollard* that ſtood leaning,
What that was writ for, and the meaning?
Hoa told me, that they was ---- a *Tu---d*;
Now I've forgot it ev'ry word.
No matter, ſo much I can tell ye,
One may be taught there all things well'y.
That * *Schools* to learn ye *conjuring*,   * *Aſtronomy School.*
* 'Tother to *Whiſtle*, and to *Sing*,   * *Muſick School.*
And how to *play* upon the *Fiddle*,
To keep the *Lads* from being idle.
But what to greater *good* amounts,
A * *School* they have to teach *Accounts*;   * *Arithmetick School.*
By which each one may caſt up nearly,
How many *Farthings* he ſpends yearly.

A *Door* I spy'd was open standing,
I budg'd no farther then my *Band in;*
But by a *Scollard* I was holp in,
A *civil Youth,* and a well spoken;
We went together up the *Stair Case,*
Going, till coming to a * *rare place,*   * Library.
As thick of *Books* as one could thatch 'um,
And *Ladders* stood about to reach 'um.
On each side were two * *round things* standing,
Made so to turn about with handing: * Two Globes
By * *one* they knew, as I am told,   * cœlstial
When Weather would be whot or cold,
What time for *setting,* and for *sowing,*
When to *prune Trees* the best for growing;
By this they make the *Almanacks,*
And twenty other harder knacks;
And 'tis by this they conjure too *Man,*
Knowing *a Thief* from any *true Man.*
So that you'd think ths *Devil's* in 'um,
Goods lost, or stole again to bring 'um;

                                And

And tho' a good while I have feen it,
I ne're can count you half, that's in it.   * *Terreftrial.*
The * other thing when round it's whurld,
Shews all the Roads about the World,
May find if well you look about,
There all the *Ponds* and *Rivers* out;
But that the *Schollard* was in hafte fo,
Hoa wou'd have fhewn our Houfe at laft too.
So I went all about the *Meeting,*
Some People in their *Pews were* * *fitting*   * *Schollars*
Tho' but a few, here and there one,   *at Study.*
The Minifter not being come;
I'le fay't, I long'd to hear the *Preaching,*
I warran't'ee, ay, *'twas dainty Teaching.*
I ask'd a *young Youth* what it mean'd,
That all them *Conjuring Books are chain'd:*
Hoa faid they being full of *Cunning,*
It feems would elfe have * been for running,
Before they had them *Chains,* they fay,   * *Or Stolen.*
A number of them run away.
There's fuch an *Ocean* ftill, I wonder'd,
How they could mifs a *thousand hunder'd.*

                                        But

But that indeed again is something,
They can know all things by the *round thing.*

As I went on, the * Folk that reads, †students disturbed.
Would many times *pop up their Heads.*
And douck 'um down (may hap) again,
And these are call'd the Learned Men.
And look for all the World as frighted,
But were I to be *hang'd, or knighted,*
I can't imagine what mought ail'd 'um,
For could they think one wou'd a *steal'd 'um;*
Well, by and by, there's one comes to me,
I thought the Fellow might have knew me,
Hoa said, I must not make a *stomping,*
And that it was no place to *jump* in ;
Whop Sir, thought I, and what ado's here,
About the Nails that in ones Shoes are;
Hoa told me that the Men were earning,
A world of something by their Learning,
And that a Noise might put them out,
So that they ne're could bring't about.

Well

Well, caufe hoa *made a din about 'um.*
I daff'd my *Shoes, and went without 'um.*
The Fellow ∥ *gern'd,* (and cry'd,) what's that for?
(I faid,) *and what would you be at,* Sir? ∥ *or fmil'd.*
My Shoes I take under *my Arm,*
Rather than do their Worfhips harm,
Becaufe I would not leave the room,
Before the Minifter be come.
At that, hoa laugh'd ; fo for my part,
I thought the Fool would break his Heart,
I vvas fo mad to fee 'n flout ma,
I long'd almoft to lay about ma ;
But thinking that might there be Evil,
I thought 'tvvere better to be civil :
Tying my Shoes upon my Feet,
I vvent dovvn Stairs into the Street.
(*Says Betty*) vvell, and prithee *John,*
Of vvhat Religion is this Tovvn ?
No, no, (Says *Tom,*) but firft let's hear,
What elfe, is to be feen there :
No more haft, then good fpeed, (cries *John,*)
I fhall be vvith you all anon ;

The

The next place that I comes you in,
Was a moſt lovely *ſpacious* thing,
To know the Name, is no great matter;
But now I think on't, 'tis the * *Thatter*,   * *Theater.*
The *Thatter* Yard about beſet is,
With *Holly*, and with *Iron Lattice*,
The ends of which, ſame Bars made faſt are,
In *Poſts* of Stone or *Alablaſter*,
And upon every *Poſtes* top,
There's an Old Mans Head ſet up;
About there ſtand a many ‖ *brave Stones*,   ‖ *Antiquities brought from Jeruſal. &c.*
Which are for all the *World like Grave-Stones*,
I marle why they were carry'd there!
No *Folks* belike are buried there.
The Houſe is round---our Maſter has,
You know, a *Round-Houſe* in the *Cloſe*;
This is much ſuch another Building,
But for the *Painting* and the *Guilding*,
The leading on the top, and then too,
'Tis twenty times as big agen too;
A top of all's a little ‖ *Steeple*,   ‖ *Cupilo.*
But ne're a *Bell to call the People*.

                                    Down

Down in the Cellar ‖ folks are doing ‖ *Printers.*
Something that makes a world of bowing,
Some throw *Black Balls*, their *Heads* some throwing,
As if they Arse-ward were a mowing,
Stooping a little more to view 'um,
They kindly ask'd me to come to 'um;
But look ye (*Tom*) for here's the thing now,
One could not come in at the Window,
And for my share, I could no more
Fly in the Air, than find the door;
A world of Paper there was lying,
Besides a deal as hung a drying,
They being wet as I suppose,
Were hung on Lines, as we hang Cloaths;
The Folk below began to hollow,
Whop, you there, honest Country Fellow ;
We'll print your Name, What is't I wonder ?
Says I, one's *John* (Sir,) t'other *Blunder*;
They bid me walk that way a little,
I'de find a *dore* about the middle :
Which having found, (said they,) *Go in,*
Not saying any kind of thing ;

E.

Well,

Well, in comes **I**, where *Men* were picking,
Of little things, that makes a nicking
And hoa that fent me, not to cheat ma,
Came up, as I came in, to meet me,
Hoa told me, *them fmall things were Letters;*
And that the Men themfelves were Setters ;
And fo would you think it ! why, this fame too,
Bid one o'th *Fellows* do my *Name* too :
And fo'a did, and down we went,
To have *John Blunder* put in *Prent ;*
And here 'tis for you all to look on't,
See, if they have not made a *Book* on't ;
Look, Look, (cryes *Befs,*) *fo 'tis I vow !*
John Blunder, *as I live 'tis fo.*
But hold, let's read the reft on't tho ;
Let *Tom,* he's the beft *Scollard* ho :
John being juft come from *Oxford,* too
Moft thought, that beft his *Name* he knew,
Having feen how 'twas put together,
They knew he could not mifs on't neither ;
So out he read it in a *Tune,*
John Blunder, Oxford Printed June :

                                                    But

But coming to the *Figures,* was
(But that *Tom* help'd him) at a loss,
Not knowing vvhat i'th' vvorld to do,
To knovv if that vvas *one* or *two* ;
At laft 'tvvas found to be *One Thoufand
Six Hundred, Seventy* and a *dozen.*
(Says *John,*) the *Printers* are fuch *Sots,*
This bit of *Paper* coft *two Pots,*
Befide, it coft me *two Pence* more,
To one that fits to || dup 'a dore, || *Open.*
That is, quite (as it vvere) vvithin there,
Where one fees all that's to be feen there ;
So, in vvent I, vvith this fame *Maiden,*
And not till I come out I paid 'en ;
It is the fineft place, that ever
My *Eyes beheld,* it's vvrought fo clever :
The || top's all *pictur'd* moft compleatly, || *The Roof of
the Theatre.*
Squar'd into *Golden Frames* fo neatly ;
Why, there is dravvn a power of things,
Nay, I dare fay, they all are Kings,
Dreft up in *Silken Garments* finely,
Some look ye *foure,* and fome look *kindly* ;

There's some kiss some, may hap a *Drab* there,
Speaks a *Wench* fine, she gives a stab there,
There's some a fighting, ones a wooing,
With little *Boys* a flying to him :
There's ‖ one looks *grinning*, welle'e *mad*,   ‖ *Envy.*
With Eels, all done about her *Head*,
She taps *Folks* till their *Blood* runs out 'um,
With all their *Guts* hanging about 'um;
There's Seats on purpose built (they say there,)
For *Folks* to sit on, they as may there : -
There is a *Gallery* made just so,
As that is in our *Church* you know.
Bess asking, What there might be done in't ?
John said, *'Twas built to look upon it,*
And that the Scollards might at leisure,
Sit there, and smoke, and take their pleasure.
Says *Tom*, Those who sit higher up,
I warr'ntee care not much to smoke.
And so—ay so, says *John,* (says he,)
For them they built the Gallery ;
That they the better might look up,
And mind the Babies at the top,

And

And to say truth, Tom, *I had rather,*
See that, then smoke a month together;
So, when I paid, I ask'd the Woman,
Which was the next place to go to, mum;
She ask'd me, *if I ever was,*
Oh! such a develish Name it has, ‖   ‖*The Laboratory*
These ugly hard words vex me more, then ---
---Well, say it is at the next dore then;
And there it is, she says, *she's sure,*
There is a world of fine things more,
But that the baster'd was not willing,
To let me in under a Shilling,
I swear, I would have given a Groat,
To please my mind, with all my heart;
But 'cause the plaguy Dog was crass,
I turn'd, and bid 'en kiss mine A---;
But being pretty late, and so,
And I not knowing where to go,
So, I went home, and went to bed,
And snor'd till morning, like one dead;
Well, up I gets, and having quaff'd,
A two quarts mug, my morning Draught;

I had

I had a swinging mind to go,
And hear the Organs you must know :
And Land-lord said, as one might hear 'um,
At Christ-Church, *which was pretty near one,*
Who e're knows Oxford, *'tis not far,*
My Horse being set up at the Star.

I thought I'de as good slip o're one day,
Look ye, because this same was *Sunday* ;
For my share, I was loth to choose,
That day to go a seeking *Shows.*
But, going down to *Queens,* to see
If my *Young Master* well might be ;
And passing over ‖ *Carryfox,*   ‖ Carfax.
Which is the *Market-place* of Ox----
Ford, where two little *Pigmys* stands,
Such *nimble-twiches* of their *Hands* ;
Just o're the place where *Folks* sell *Butter,*
And with two *Hammers* keep a clutter ;
It being their business (so belike,)
To knock, when e're the Clock shall strike,

A

A *Bell*, that's hung ye fo between,
That fo, they might befure to fee'n;
Alive, fure as a *band*, a *band* is,
With *Heads* no bigger then ones *hand* is,
As long---lets fee, if *I* can tell now, ---
About as long as from my *Elbow*,
Elfabeth faid, *She met a Fairy*
One morning early in the Dairy:
Cries *John*, *Juft fuch a one 'twas* Betty,
Such Folks I vow are very pretty.
Why, I've feen too *New-Colledge* mount,
And ftood ye a good while upon't;
And *Maudling walks*, and *Chrift-Church* Fountain,
A thing that makes a mighty fprounting:
Well, *Monday* comes, and hardly neither,
Before *Day-break* I hies me thither;
But I found out by Peoples faying,
Thefe *Organs* would not yet be playing.
And that I might go home again,
And come and hear 'um juft at Ten;
By then the *Bells* had all done ringing,
The *Folks* were come, and fet a finging,

　　　　　　　　　　　　　　　　There's

There's fome are *fat*, and fome are *lean*,
And fome are *Boys* and fome are *Men*,
But what I'me fure will make you ftare,
They all ftand in their ‖ *Shirts* I fwear ; ‖ *furplicet.*
Here *Sufan* blufh'd, and *John* befeeches,
To tell, if thefe all wore no *Breeches.*
Cries *John*, that one can hardly know,
They wear their *Linnen* things fo low ;
Each one when they come in, ftand ftill,
Bowing, and wrigling at the Sill ;
I look'd a while, and mark'd one *Noddy*,
‖ Something he bow'd to, but no *Body*, ‖ *The Altar*
For thefe and other things as *apifh*,
The *Town-folks* term the *Scollards* Papifh ;
The *Organs* fet up with a *ding*,
The *White-men* roar, and *White-Boys* fing,
Rum, *Rum*, the Organs go, and *did*,
Sometimes they *fqueek* out like a *Pig*,
Then *gobble* like a *Turky Hen*,
And then to *Rum*, *Rum*, *Rum* again :
What with the *Organs*, *Men*, and *Boys*,
It makes ye up a *difmal Noife*;

                                        All

All being over as I wifs,
Out come they like a *Flock* of *Geefe*.

   The *place* as I went in at, there
A kind of *Yat-houfe*, as it were ;
A top of which a *Bell* is hung,
Bigger than e're was look'd upon,
I underftood by all the *People*,
'Twas bigger than our *Church* and *Steeple* ;
At *Nine* at night, it makes a *Bomeing*,
And then the *Scollards* all muft come in.

   Now I've told all that e're I fee,
Unlefs the *brazen Nofe* it be,
Clapt on a *College Yat* to grace it,
And fhew, may hap, they're *brazen Faced* ;
And there's another thing I think on,
The *Devil* looking over *Lincoln* ;
Their *Faults* befure, he kindly winks on,
Tho other *Colleges* he fquints on ;

A world of pity 'twas, I swear,
That our *Young Master* was not there.

   Bess willing, yet to be more knowing,
Demands *what Clothes Schollars go in?*
For the most part (says *John,*) they wear
Such kind of *Gowns* as *Parsons* are ;
Some *Trenchers* on their *Heads* have got,
As black as yonder *Perridge-Pot* ;
And some have things, exactly such
As my *Old Gammers* mumbles *Pouch,*
Which sits upon his Head as neat,
As 'twere sew'd to't by e'ry *Pleat :*
Some I dare say, are very poor, tho
They wear their *Gowns* berent and tore so,
Hanging about them all in *Littocks,*
That they can hardly hide their *Buttocks.*
When they want *Mony,* I believes,
The *Lads* are fain to sell their *Sleeves,*
Because they have their stunt of *Victuals,*
And that I'me sure, but very little's ;

For

For look ye, *many a time I meet,*
May *happen twenty in the Street,*
With handſome Gowns *to look upon,*
And ne'r *a Sleeve to all their Gowns.*
You know Young Maſter *for a Meater,*
Was ſor his Years *a handſome Eater* ;
Well, *and his Sleeves are gone already,*
And his was *a New Gown too,* Betty,
And hangs about his Legs *in ſhatters,*
I ſwear, *'has torn it all to tatters.*
I held a jag aloft, *to ſhew'n,*
And bid'n let the Taylor ſew'n.
Hoa laught, and cry'd, Why, that's no fault *John,*
Hoa tor't, to paſs ye for a * Saltman ;　　* senior.
But I have ſometimes met with ſome
Young Men, *may chance with a* whole Gown,
Holding 'um out as if they'd *dry* 'um,
So that one hardly can get by 'um.
Cry'd Tom, *So drunk they could not miſs 'um,*
What naſty Dogs they're to *be-piſs 'um.*
Cry'd John, *No, vvhile they have a Govvn,*
They make uſe of their time to ſhevv'n.

F 2　　　　　　　　Now

Now you have all, let's go to *Bed*,
I well'y long to lay my *Head:*
And *John* that motion made, becauſe
Their *Eyes* by this time all drew *Stravvs* ;
All thank him round, *Sue*, *Beſs*, and *Tom*,
And went to Rooſt all ev'ry one.

Now *John* has done his *Banbury Story*,
With no ſmall *Pride* or little *Glory*,
Beſide a luſty *Toſt* and *Ale*,
As ſoon as he had done his *Tale*,
Which *Tale*, if you too ſoon forget it,
I vow, I ſhould be ſtrangely fretted ;
I ſhould not ſtand ſo much upon it,
But that my *Tale* depends ſo on it ;
That if this *John* ſhould be left out,
I know not how to bring't about :
Alas ! I ſhould be very willing,
To give full fourty round broad Shilling,
To tell a *Tale* as well as he,
And purchaſe ſuch a *Memory*;

But

But 'cauſe I'de have you think me honeſt,
I ſhall go back, ſo as I promis'd.

I think I brought them up to *Town*,
And ſtaid till all their *Coin* was gone:
Their *Needs* by this time has bereft 'um,
Of the bare *ſcent* on't, all I left 'um;
By this time, *Maſter* has forgot,
His Mothers *Sweet-meats* for a *Pot*,
And the *Pack-rider* (ſuch another)
Loves a *Girl* better than his *Mother*,
Being much of a *Faculty*,
In general, they much agree,
To ſcrub all day, a *Nut-brown Table*,
With all the might, as they are able;
From hence it is, that ſome poor *Fellows*
Have ſo thin *Cloathing* at their *Elbows*.
In this *Opinion* I am bold,
Becauſe the *Reaſon* is two-fold.
For here they ſpend their *Wits* and *Coin* too,
In getting *nothing*, ſpend their *time* too;

And

And tho, they take so much *Delight*
To make their *Landlord*'s *Table* bright,
And wear their *Gowns* and *Elbows* out,
In labouring to bring't about ;
Seldom their *Hostess* so befriends 'um,
To *mend*, or pay the *Man* that mends 'um.
Now what will *Mothers Hony* do,
Depriv'd of *Cloaths* and *Mony* too ;
But send by * *Basset*, or *John Hickman*,   * *Carrier.*
A *Line*, to make his *Friends* more quick *Man*,
That he's in a most *sad Condition*,
Worse I believe, than *Nick* could wish him,
And that he wants more *Mony*, so
He knows not what i'th world to do ;
Hopes they're well, as at this sending
He is, and so he falls to ending.
Now if his *Friends* are *poor*, or *witty*
Enough to fain they're so, or * *Nitty*,   * *close-Fisted.*
For want of *Mony*, to say truth,
Most an end makes a *hopeful Youth* :
But those who count by *Pocket-fulls*,
Empt *them* together with their *Sculls*,

                                        To

To a *Hat-full* of *Head*, 'tis fair,
If *Brains* a *Thimble-full* be there,
Enough to practice by a *Sample*,
How they may pass for *Schollars* ample ;
In spight of *vacant Heads*, and *Hours*,
Half *Gowns* are always *Seniours*,
So halv'd and jag'd, if needs you'l know,
If *Seniour Soph* 'has *Govvn* or no ;
Looking on's *Shoulders*, and no lower,
Perhaps it may be in your power.
When they've been there about a *Quarter*,
Say half a *Year*, or such a matter,
Their *Friends* think it more orderly
To send their *Mony* quarterly ;
By this time, they have more occasion
For *Ready*, than the poor o'th *Nation*,
Thinking they better know the use on't,
A *Peer* o'th *Realm* is less profuse on't ;
That *Week* o'th *Quarter*, as they have it,
He's damn'd with *them* who thinks to save it :
Now for that *necessary Trick*,
To *book*, and *score*, and *run a Tick*,

For

For *Govvn*, and *Cap*, for *Drink*, and *Smoke*,
And so much more for *Ink*, and *Chalk*;
Five pound a *Coat*,----- *Ink* Five more-----Ten,
Six Bottles, ---- *Chalk* as much agen;
A *Glass* broke; *Six pence* ---- so much more,
Because 'twas put upon the *Score*.
And at this rate the *Coxcombs* run
Their *Daddies* out of *House* and *Home*;
Those that in *Debt*, the least may be,
Perhaps owe Hundreds two, or three,
Till fallen downright *sick* of *Duns*,
Keeps Chamber, till the *Carrier* comes;
The *ready Mony*, when they send it,
He must upon his *Mistress* spend it;
And so that very *Night* he runs
To honest *Joan* of *Hed---tons*,
Who brags she has been a *Beginner*
With many an after-harden'd *Sinner*;
As to a *Book* an *Introduction's*
To *Vice*, so she, and her *Instruction's*;
And since the *Doctrine* of her *School's*
Practis'd, and follow'd so by *Fool's*,

                                For

For pray, in all our *Modern Hist'ries*,
Look me a *Fool without a Mistriss*.
Whose part's to set the *Gins*, and bait 'um,
And the snare'd Ideot's part, to treat 'um,
So *Schollars*, who do all ☞ Rules,
without Example, won't be Fools,
And dedicate their ready Monies,
To please, and to divert their Honies;
Not, that they're given all to whoreing,
Some are for *honest dovvnright roaring*;
And quite another sort of Fellows,
Love nothing but a noise, and *Ale-House*:
I would not have you here mistake me;
I know not how, 'tis you may take me,
Ne're think think these *Youngsters, by their looks,*
Will mate their Heads, *with silly Books*:
Which a *Cann-Lover* minds no more,
Then he that loves an ugly *Whore,*
Being none but Ugly in the Town,
Since one *Mal's* dead, and t'other gone;
The Lads content are in their Room,
To Court a *Moppstick,* or a *Broom,*

G

Drest

Dreſt in a *Night-Rail,* and a *Settee,*
Dear *Nancy* call it, and their *Betty,*
But then, he makes a hideous quarter,
If once ammomer'd on's *Taylors Daughter;*
You may then, at the ſame Church ſee him,
Which Father, Mother, has, and ſhe in
Coming out, down he vales his *Bonnet,*
And next day *pelts her with a Sonnet;*
But if ſhe ſtubborn chance to prove,
He makes a *Changeling of his Love,*
And in a ſtrange Poetick Ire,
Grows very *Smutty, very dire,*
As ſharp as may be, to ſay truth,
Seeing his Muſe had ne're a Tooth;
And heretofore, 'twas no great matter,
For Teeth to any private Satyr;
But now let each look to his Brawls,
And not refer't to Generals;
Since now, there wants a publick *Prater,*
To raiſe the *Hiſs,* or *Hum oth' Theater,*
Such as we took for *Owls, and no Men,*
Who knew not how t' abuſe the *Women,*

'Twas

'Twas then, no more, *but let some Lad*,
Highly diſturb'd, and Vengeance mad,
Where the *Girl* gave juſt cauſe, or no,
Let him, to *Terræ Filius go*:
'Twas he, knew how to mak't appear,
As true, as you alive ſtand there,
Wiſe *Sparks*, and bold, who durſt to tell them,
Their Faults, who could, and did expell them.
But theſe mad *whipſters*, have given o're now,
And laſh theſe, and the *Town no more now.*
The Act, a time they did all this at,
Is ſtill a time as much to hiſs at,
At which time, when ſo e're it comes,
Wiſe Men of *Gotham,* change their Gowns,
Which is a kind of Term, d'ee ſee,
I uſe for taking a Degree.
Having had other things to follow,
They pray their *Chum,* or *Chamber-Fellow,*
To help them out to ſay their part,
For want of time to get't by heart;
For here the Miſery of it lies,
When they're oblig'd to exerciſe,

G 2

Which

Which is, e're they take a Degree,
Some *Fellow*, or what e're he be;
Asks him if things be *so*, or *so*,
To which he answers ay, or no,
And if he happens to say right,
He gets ye his Degree, in spight
Of *Lousie Learning*, to which end,
Some better Scholar, and his Friend,
H'intreats, because he would not miss,
To hold his Finger up at *Yes*;
And when his turn comes to say *no*,
To do his finger *so*, or *so*.

And now no question, but you'l ask   ¶*Sunday.*
How 'tis, they so neglect their Task,
Folks can't do all at once, for look, Sir,
They've more to do, than con a Book, sure,
For *Sundays* work, it very fare is,
To see, who preaches at St. *Maries*,
Peep in at *Carfax Church*, to see there,
Either who preaches, or what *she there* :

Then

Then, as if troubled with the *Squitters,*
Away they feque it to, St. *Peters,*
When up into the *Chancel* coming,
Which moft an end is full of *Women,*
About they ftrut a while, and feek out,
And one vouchfafe at laft, to pick out,
Or cry; *pox, ne're a handfome Woman* :
And *Preacher being in Prayer Common* ;
They can't a while fo long to ftay,
To fee who Preaches there to day:
So, in their way down to *St. Giles,*
For more difpatch, they take St. *Miles,*
'Caufe they're oblig'd, e're Church be done,
To thruft their Nofe in every one;
Which makes them run, *and fweat, and Blurry,*
And puts them in the deadlieft hurry,
For 'tis you know, a *Common* faying,
Bufinefs admits of no delaying.

When coming to the *Quaker's Meeting,*
Where fome are ftanding, fome are fitting,

Eyes

Eyes fhut, with open Mouths, *fome lunging,*
Amidft the *Brother-hood*, they *fcrunge in,*
Approaching of a handfome *Sifter,*
With her Eyes clofed, make bold to kifs her ;
Which mov'd her *Sponfe,* but never mov'd her,
Taking him for a *Friend* that lov'd her ;
But her *Friend John,* fuppos'd that he,
Beftow'd no Kifs of Charity ;
Which made *his Gutts for madnefs, wamble,*
Friend (fays he) *giving him a jumble,*
Do thou, I fay, let her alone,
Or elfe, 'twere better thou wert gone ;
Do fo, in thy own *Steeple-Houfe,*
And not in other Peoples Houfe.
To which the Schollar anfwers, *rat it,*
What makes the Fellow fo mad at it.
He wonders what the *Quaker thinks* on't,
'Twas done to her, and ftill fhe winks on't.

But Quack flips out to tell the *Procter,*
How Schollars kift his Wife, *and mock'd her;*

At

At our Aſſembly, hard by here,
The Young Men ſtill (I'me ſure) are there ;
So I made haſte to come to thee,
That thou might'ſt come thy ſelf and ſee :
Since 'tis thy buſineſs to protect 'um,
Prithee do thou therefore -correct 'um.
After this *Speech* the *Proctor* coming,
Sets all the *Crew* of *Royſters* running,
And upon *all* he lays his *Hands,*
He either takes *them* or their *Gowns ;*
And he's glad on't with all his heart,
Who gets off with his *Gown* in part,
Not being a thing accounted ſhameful,
To have's *Govvn* leſſen'd by a handful,
Since all the *puniſhment* and *ſhame*
Light's only on the *Fools,* are ta'ne ;
Like *Birds,* put in a *Cage* to whiſle,
Unleſs they patch up an *Epiſtle,*
To'th *Proctor,* for the which he looks,
Beſure in every one, one's *Books,*
Fills his *Head,* full as ere't can hold,
Becauſe e're long they muſt be ſold ;

Monday.

Thrum-

Thrumming out several *scraps* of *Latin*,
As like as *Dowvlas* is to *Satin* :
An expeditious way, and better
Then make of his own *head*, a *Letter*,
Or wanting *Books* to tumble o're,
He gets a *Letter* made before ;
Hackney Epistle to the *College*,
For those who have but little *knowvledge* ;
No sooner this the *Proctor* sees,
But his *offence* he strait forgives,
For joy of which, he roars most deadly,
And sails that afternoon to medly,
Near half a mile, or such a matter,
It lyes as you go down the Water ;
A place at which they never fail,
Of *Custard, Cyder, Cakes,* and *Ale,*
Cream, Tarts, and *Cheese-Cakes,* good *Neats Tongues,*
And pretty *Girls* to wait upon's.

Schollars by right in studying Hours,
Or should not late be out of Doors,

                                        But

But having found with how much eafe,
At worft the *Proctor* they appeafe,
And long e're this, and for the future,
Knowing how to fatisfy their *Tutor*.
Some *Country Stranger*, or a *Brother*,
Some *Friend Relation* or another,
Being come to *Town* only to ftare,
Will be a *Week* or *Fortnight* here;
And he can do no lefs, than go
Sometimes to wait on him, or fo,
Treat him, go with him up and down,
At leaft, and fhew him all the *Town* :
That he at home might tell a *Story*,
O'th *Theatre* and *Labo'ratory*.
And ever when one *Strangers* gone,
Befure they'l have another come;
And then you know, it would be evil,
If they to *Strangers* be uncivil;
And then fometimes their *Father* fends,
Or elfe fome other of their *Friends*,
(They fay,) a *Letter* of *Attorney*,
Praying them to take a little *Journey*,

H   To

To such a *Town* near *two hours* going,
To take some *Money* they have owing ;
The *Postscript* runs, *Dear Son* or *Cozen*,
Make haste to go, or else you'l lof'en.

When *Tuesday* comes, he's up by *Noon*,   *Tuesday.*
Least *Doufon*'s *dancing* should be done,
'Cause he'd be there, he very fairly
Forsakes his *Bed* so very early.
Tho he sate up the *Night* before,
To smoke his *Bed—mat*, for the Dore
By *Nine*, is always so fast shut,
That no *Soul* living can get out.
As for *Tobacco* he'd forgot it,
Tho e'ry *Night* he us'd to fot it,
And so was fain to *do as a' could*,
Because he *cou'd not do as he would*.
And truth, they care not one should know it,
But they're as poor as any *Poet* :
Fortune, that Enemy to *sense* is,
She makes *Fools* poor for bare *Pretences*.

                                    And

And tho to smoke they're so *Delighted*,
They want wherewith to *Pot* and *Pipe* it,
And so all Night, *They* and their *Chums*,
Sit whiffing *Straws* till morning comes;
And then betake them to their *Beds*,
And *lye* till *Four* to ease their *Heads:*
But being oblig'd to come to *Prayers*,
Whipping the *Surplice* o're their *Ears*;
At *Six* some places, some at *Ten*,
To *Prayers*, that done, to *Bed* again.

　　Wednesday being come *six Hours* ago,　*Wednesday.*
He's up, and say, he's ready too;
Forsooth, he rose that day so rare,
Because he'd take the *Country Air.*
Perhaps some *Fools* rise more betimes,
And meet with but *unwholesome Rimes*,
Which for the *World* they would not go in,
From *Letters* Schollars are so knowing;
Now for their *way* of going a *shooting*,
Sometimes a *Horse-back*, sometimes *Footing:*

　　　　　　　　Approach-

Approaching some *Lone House*, or *Cottage*,
Reaking with *Bacon*, *Herbs* and *Pottage*,
Ne're *knock*, but *baul* out, *Who's within there?* ——
Who's there? —— *two or three come to dine here.*
Then *Jenny* coming out in *Kersey*,
Makes to the *Gentle Folks* a *Cursey*;
Her *Mother* calling from within,
Jane, bid the *Gentlefolk* come in;
In they come, *Welcome by her Troth*,
Who freely sets them all she hath;
Glad in their hearts, that *Folks* so brave,
Will please to eat all they have.
Can you eat in a homely *Tray?*
You're welcome all as I may say.
They've done, but having other *Butts*,
Beside the stuffing of their *Gutts*.
Jane going for to'ther *Pot* of *Ale*,
They seldom of a flitching fail;
The *Mother* sometimes going after,
To wring the *Tap* in for her *Daughter*, &c
The while they get it from the rack,
And take their leaves when she comes back,

The

The good Wife vexing, can't but think,
'Tis ftrange they would not ftay, and drink!
But then fhe's in a woful taking,
When once fhe comes to mifs her *Bacon.*
But fhe's in as much *woe agen,*
For lofing of her fpeckled Hen;
The Scholars, as for their parts, they
Go home rejoicing in their Pray;
And at the very next *Farmers door,*
Shoot two or three Ducks, and Pullets more;
Thus being provided of good Victles,
Their next care is to wet their *Whifles,*
Contriving where 'twere beft to feat 'um,
And of the beft way to defeat 'um;
Becaufe as I before was faying,
They've bitterly againft all Paying;
So having call'd for what they will,
And yauld, and fung, and drunk their fill;
Going forth as to untrufs a Point,
They run their Legs near out of Joint,
'Till they have reached the Town agen,
And fome fuch other * *bowzing Ken,*   * *Ale-houfe.*

Playing

Playing a world of *pretty Knacks,*
As oft as People turn their backs,
Melt the Folks Flagons, burn their Bellows,
Then sear a loft their Names 'ith' Ale-house.
And in their Breeches put their Candles,
The Snuffers and the Flaggon handles.

Next Morning raging Hostess comes   *Thursday.*
To's Chamber door with other Duns:
There's such a *din* and such a *drumming,*
As if the King of *France* was coming:
As if their Business were to keep him
And all the *College* too from sleeping.
Then sometimes hold their hands for cunning,
And lend an ear to hear him coming;
Because if he should think them gone,
He would *peep out* twenty to one.
Their patience tir'd, to't they *go,*
Ran dan, tara ran, clutter to quo.
Are you within, Sir, Mr. Snear——
Yes that he is, and knows who's there,

Knows

Knows all your Voices, great and small,
And to the Devil sends ye all.

Casting an Eye, *first thro' a Chink,*
One of his Neighbours *fitting think,*
To open gingerly the door,
Because he is not very sure,
But that some *Ambuscade might fire,*
Before the *neatly could retire,*
Having by this judicious care,
Perceiv'd the Coast all round him clear,
That every individual Dun,
His Neighbours are, and not his own;
He with a Noble Courage speaks,
And to them thus his mind he breaks,
Sirs, if you'd speak with Mr. *Snear,*
You must not think to find him there;
He went abroad Three hours ago,
And goes out ev'ry morning so;
But Sir, tho now he b'en't within,
Pray when, de'e think, he will come in?

When

When he goes out by three or four,
He comes not in 'till ten, or more:
Because his busineſs will not let him,
I wonder that you never met him:
If with him you'd ſo fain a' ſpoken,
You ſhould come e're the Gates are open.
They thank him for his gracious Speeches,
And then toward him turn their *Breeches*,
Going their ways, tak't for a warning,
To come more early the next Morning.

Now *Snear* releas'd thus of his Cares,
Tells all his *Duns down all the ſtairs.*
Before he's very ſure he's ſafe,
He dare not wry his Mouth to laugh.
Truely, there comes a deal of good,
From *Fellowfeeling Neighbourhood!*
T'other comes to *Congratulate,*
With him the goodneſs of his Fate,
Who thro' the *Key-hole looks to ſee him,*
And asks if there no more be we'him,

Aſſur'd

Aſſur'd he's *Solus*, to be ſhort,
Comes boldly out, and thanks him for't.

But now it being *dinner time*,
They venture to the *Hall to dine*,
Where *Baxter*, one that *lets out Horſes*,
Comes, hoping to repair his Loſſes;
And being wiſer than the reſt,
Thinks there to find his Debters beſt,
Who mind their *Cramming*, but not ſo,
But they've an Eye for ſuch a Foe,
Contriving, *Dinner done, to tumble*
Together, all out in a Bundle;
Deceiving thus his Vigilance;
Who to repair this great miſchance,
Setting up's Throat, begins to hollow it,
Sir, Sir, why Sir, there, Mr. *Shallow-wit*;
But as for Mr. *Shallow-wit*, *he*
Has more wit, than to hear or ſee,
So in the Crow'd, away he goes,
And nothing of the matter knows:

I   *Creditor*

Creditor doubts if that might be him,
Or elſe concludes he did not ſee him ;
And ſince 'tis ſo the *bubbl'd Dun*,
Contented as he can, goes home.

'Twere to be wonder'd why the *Townſ-men*,
Have ſo much fooliſh Faith for *Gownſ-men*,
But here the Myſtery of it lies,
Theſe ſeeming Fools, are truly wiſe,
For if they can by all their comings
To Hall, and Chambers, all their dunnings,
Their horrid threats, that *for the future,*
They'l come no more, but tell their Tutor.
Or of ſome piece of Merriment,
To tell the Head, or *Preſident.*
If by theſe Arts he clears one ſcore,
He can ſuſtain the loſs of four :
And he that to be honeſt chooſes ;
In paying, pays him all he looſes.
So that the Trader might afford it,
To loſe the reſt, and never word it ;

But

But that your Merchants ever love,
Something to gain o're and above.

Always when once 'tis Afternoon,
Duns with the *Colleges* have done;
And Scholars *looking well about*,
With caution, venture to go out;
For many times it happens so's,
I'th' very face *to meet their Foes*:
With Sir, *you know you owe me, for*
Maintaining of *your Spotted Cur*;
*I'*me sure, I bought him as good *Meat*,
As any *Christian,* Sir, *could eat*:
If there's in Man any Belief,
I always fed the Whelp with Beef;
A deal of Money, *I disburst so,*
And *Money* going out of *Purse* so---
*I'*de ask'd your *Tutor,* but to stay me,
You said, that you'd next *Quarter pay me,*
'Las *I'*me a *poor Man,* that you know,
And yet you'l *never pay me too*.

The *Sparks so thunder-struck at this,*
He hardly can tell what he is,
Protests to *Harry,* he is willing
To pay, bids him, *here, take that shilling,*
Being all he has now in his Pocket,
As for his Chest he can't unlock it,
Because he has either spoil'd his *Key,*
Lost it, or laid it out o'th' way;
And says, when e're he comes for the rest,
He'll pay him, or *he'll break his Chest.*
These words give *Harry* Satisfaction
Beyonde th'event, or *threaten'd Action;*
Who fancies in this *Chest a Mint,*
When there is ne're a penny in't.

    Therefore to shun such Brunts as these,
Scholars in *walking cross the Ways,*
Ne're grutching Shoo-leather, or ground,
For more convenience circle round,
And many times set up a running,
And all for fear of Duns, and dunning;

                                        Let

Let their *Walk* for *Example* this be,
To *Weavers School*, from *Corpus Christi* :
Thro' *Christ-Church*, *Penny-farthing Street*,
Where there lives none he fears to meet ;
His way down by St. *Thomas* lyes,
And so he slips by *Paradice*,
And falls to running there from going,
Least any should come out as know him,
Because he owes them for his *Custard*,
Nor paid yet for his *Tongue*, and *Mustard* ;
Tho once being took, he made a *promise*.
From *Castle-Bridge*, up from St. *Thomas* :
Thro *Bullocks-Lane*, unsight, unseen,
He's like a *spright* in *Gloufter-Green*,
From thence he goes out by St. *Giles's*,
And thro' the *Fields* which near a *mile* is,
Yet by then *twenty* you could tell,
He's arriv'd safe in *Holy-well* ;
And when you're come about the middle,
You may know *Weavers* by the *Fiddle* ;
A *Boarding*, and a *Dancing School*,
Where *People* learn to go by *Rule*,

                                        And

And 'tis high time he there fhould be,
It being fomething now paft *Three*;
To be there's, of concern as much
To him, as going is to *Church*,
Going to *fee*, more than to *hear*;
The very fame as he does there;
Dancing being done, and *Dangers* paft,
He get's to's *College* fafe at laft:
He might by much a nearer way found,
That is, by *Maudlins*, and the *Grey-hound*,
And mift the *Town* as well; but there's
So deeply plung'd o're head and ears,
The very *Signs* enough to fright him,
Leaft the curft *Dog* in it might bite him.

Next day, when all the *Houfe* is fnoring,
Befure his *Duns* are up before him,
As if their *Souls* made up one *Song*,
The *Stairs* as by *Agreement* throng,
And fo harmoniously each one
Raps at his *Door* as in his turn;

Tho

Tho' met; but one of all thofe *Fools* there,
Knows what the benefit of *Shools* are;
He was that one, who fure as can be,
Miffing a *Bottle* of lovely *Brandy*,
And being in a world of *Dolour*,
And finding out this worthy *Schollar*;
Both too alone, for only faying,
That he defir'd that he would pay him;
Threatned for *Payment* was with *Pumping*,
And put to fave himfelf by *jumping*
O're a *Wall*, might break his *Neck*,
To keep his *Back* from being *vvet*.
'Tis fo unfafe for any *Dun*,
To 'accoft a *Schollar* all alone;
At many, tho he looks fo leering,
He'll make a fingle one to fear him:
As I before faid, I fay here,
'Tis well they are enow for *Snear*,
Beating his *Door*, they keep him waking,
And fpoil his *Peace*, as well as *Napping*.

Here

Here was his *Shoe-maker*, and *Taylor*,
His *fiery Hoftefs*, Mrs. *Rayler*;
And *Drawers* fhaking off their *Noddles*,
For loofing of their *Wine and Bottles*;
And a kind *Girl* befide, who had
Made him a *Twelve-month* fince a *Dad*;
Good reafon why fhe came to feek him,
For fomething towards the *Infants* keeping,
Among the *Croud* for *Payment* whining,
was fhe that us'd to make his *Linnen*;
Where grumbling an *Old Gardner* ftood,
Who loft his *Hedge* for *Fire-wood:*
Befide his *Rake*, his *Hoe*, and *Shovel*,
And half the *Faggots* off his *Hovel*;
And *Country-men*, amidft all thefe,
For loofing *Turkeys*, *Hens*, and *Geefe*;
Mercury was there, who on the wing, goes
To make him pay for's *Ladies Windows*;
And in his hand he bore a *Ticket*,
Demanding reafon *why he brake it* ?
His *Landrefs* having all his *Linnen*,
Need never *Dun*, or go to *Spinning*,

Wafhing,

Washing, becaufe he's fain to pay for't,
He feldom wears but half a *Day-Shirt*,
At firft fhe'l chop, and change, and choofe 'um,
And dextroufly at laft fhe'l loofe 'um,
Nor by this moft ingenious way,
Can hardly get up half her pay ;
His *Bedmaker* whilft at the *Ale-houfe*,
For *Pay* can feize his *Bed* and *Pillows*,
And for that *Reafon* is more cunning,
Then to beftow the pains to *dun* him.

The *Dunners* having hinted been,
That Mr. *Snear* was now within,
Were fully bent for very fpight,
To ftand all at his *Door* till *Night*,
And by fo clofe a *Siege* go nye they
To make him truly faft his *Friday*
No longer able to fuftain it,
No more than's *Father* to maintain it.
Snear vows to morrow he'l be going,
From all the *Noife* of *Mony* owing ;

For *Schollarship* he here forswears it,
And takes his tatter'd *Gown*, and tares it.

And now his restless *Duns* are gone,
He takes his *farewell* of the *Town*,
Meeting at *Midnight* with the *Procter*,
With less concern then if a *Doctor*,
Not only very boldly meets him,
But to return his *Question*, beats him;
Which having done, as fast he runs,
As when he us'd to meet his *Duns* :
And in his *Flight*, breaking his *Shin*, now's
Fully reveng'd on the next *Windows* ;
In which *Sport* when his hand is in,
He lays about like any thing,
Roaring, and hallowing down the *Streets*,
Swears to knock down the next he meets.
Wallowing all *Night* in such *Abuses*,
Nor studies for next days *Excuses*;
Knowing he shall complete his *Sport*
At *home*, or at the *Inns* of *Court*,

'Cause

'Caufe I'me not willing to fuppofe here,
Our *Teachers* ever fuch as thofe were.

  The *Day* now coming on a new, *Saturday.*
Wherein he bids the *Town* adieu,
Having no encouragement to tarry here,
Sends for his *Wardrobe* by the *Carrier.*
Now free at liberty and peace is,
Secure, unask'd, goes where he pleafes,
Here cruel *Duns*, nor fear'd expulfion,
Can fhake his *Soul* to a *Convulfitn,*
Bearing the *Learning* off, he's free
From all the *Plagues* o'th '*Verfity.*

No *Cæfar's* lofs lamented more yet,
Then where he us'd to *book* and *fcore* it;
The *Tears* of *Mothers*, and of *Duns,*
Hers for *loft Children*, theirs for *Sums,*
More *unconftrain'd* are, and *true,*
Then thofe I fhed in this *Adieu.*

F I N I S.

ADVERTISEMENTS.

THE Secret Intreagues of the *French King's Ministers*, at the Courts of several Princes, for the Enslaving of *Europe*. With Reflections on the Interest of those Princes. *qro.* price 1 *s.*

Buchanan's Detection of *Mary* Queen of *Scotland*, concerning the Murther of her Husband. *Quarto* price 1 *s.*

The Right of the People over *Tyrants*, by *John Milton*. *Quarto*, Price 6 *d.*

Some Modest Remarks on Dr. *Sherlock's* Case of Allegiance, &c. *Quarto*. Price 6 *d.*

All four sold by *Randal Taylor*.

THE
Oxford-Act:
A
POEM.

LONDON;
Printed for *Randal Taylor*, near *Stationers-Hall*, MDCXIII.

THE

A

POEM.

A True Relation of their Practice
At Oxford *Town when there an ACT is.*

CANTO I.

Half Choakt ith' Duft of our lewd Town,
 Tir'd with their Follies and my own ;
 To breath a Wifer Air, and better,
 With many a Token, many a Letter,
I tript to t'other *Alma Mater.*
Thoufands One, Hundreds Six, Tens Ninety,
Three Ones the Year exactly point t'ye,
When a remarkable Occafion
Brought there the Learn'd and Wife oth' Nation :
The *Act* which fome believ'd muft be
Turn'd to a *Jewifh Jubilee,*
Whofe joyful found that Nation hears
No more than Once in Fifty Years.
The *Act,* which now they difcontinue
So long, fome thought, they ne'er had any ;

But that some forward Scribes in Iniquity
Had feign'd it like their own Antiquity.
Oft wou'd the new created Sophister
Where Boy cry'd, want ye any *Coffee*, Sir ?
Start from brown-study, answering rather
When comes the *Act*, the *Act*, Dear Father ?
The Beardless Father sigh'd, but knew
No more of that than I or You ;
For all his Logick and his History,
This an unfathomable Mystery.
Even the Grave *Doctors* scarce cou'd tell
Without the help of *Chronicle*,
When last they in their Boots appear'd,
And Bugbear *Terræ-Filius* fear'd.
Now one, and then the other Faction
Putting the Dons beyond their Action:
Now *Whig*, as *Nobbs* had then bedighted him
With Horns and Tail cry'd *Bough*, and 'frighted 'em ;
Till they stark staring run with one Mouth,
To rail at, and discomfit *Monmouth*:
Tho' wiser *Cam* to save his Bacon,
His Picture kept till he was taken.
Then their Lov'd *Chancellor's* Picture banish,
As *Rome* unfortunate *Sejanus*.
More Loyal *Oxford*, *Windsor* trusted
With many a Pondrous Pike and Musket,
Soon form'd in Squadrons and Battalions
To swinge the Duke's Tatterdemalions:
But Blessings on that Noble Lord,
Who sav'd the Labour of their Sword ;
Who did the Tall-Young Man betray,
And run most Loyally away.
O happy *Oxford*! happy since
Fate gave thee such a grateful Prince ;

True

True to his Friends beyond comparifon,
He *Jefferys* fent to pay thy Garrifon;
Whofe *Mufick-Speech* fo fore did fright ye
The *Act* that Summer cry'd Good-night t'ye.
Since then, Confufion on Confufion,
All Chaos till the *Revolution*;
Till a New World rofe from black Billows,
And *Surges* roll'd as foft as Pillows.
Yet then Fate had fo long been thwarting,
So ftunn'd with the old Blows of Fortune,
The Aged Matron did appear,
She fcarce got Breath in Four long Year:
But now recover'd brisk and Bonny,
As Bridegroom's felf, in Moon-call'd-*Hony*,
An *Act* as I before have told y'it
She'll have, and all crowd to behold it.
Expect not all the Nation over
From *Cornifh Mount*, to Peer of *Dover*,
I fhou'd recite, fince did I know it,
'Twould look like *Herald*, not like *Poet*:
Then reft content with what I give ye
To further trouble fave, believe me.   *Hyperbaton.*

I'll only fing what Troops have gone down
From thee, O *Trinobantick-London*!
Three *Aldermen*, and one wife *Juftice*,
Some of the *Orphans* trufty *Truftees*.
To fhew their equal Wit and Valours
Ten *Woollen-Drapers*, Nine ftout *Taylors*,
Likewife to Vifit their Acquaintances
A well-teeth'd Band of Fifty *Prentices*.
Three Jolly *Landladies* went jogging,
Their Rofy Cheeks, confefling *Nogging*;

Their

Their Cheeks with Sweat and Gravy running,
And wot ye what--- They went a Dunning;
Some certain *Lads* that ſhall be namelefs,
(For we'd have none ſhould juſtly blame this,)
Not long ſince made an Expedition
In *Water-Poet*'s low Condition;
(For which the Rude wou'd call 'em Blockheads,)
London to ſee with empty Pockets:
On theſe kind *Hoſteſſes* they lighted,
And ſince they found themſelves not ſlighted,
Them now to ſee the *Act* invited:
Which kindnefs they accept the rather,
In hopes of *Ready-Bill* from *Father*.

I'th' Name o'th' Beadle, what ill Fortune,
Before Remembrance drew a Curtain,
That I, on theſe lewd Scholars plodding,
The Cream o'th' Jeſt had half forgotten.

Upon the Road i'th' Crowd I ſaw there
Two *Bookſellers* and One *poor Author*:
The *Author* firſt through Duſt was trudging;
With Clouted-Shoon, like *D---well* drudging;
By Sympathy I look'd upon him,
And caſt a few good Wiſhes on him,
And him behind my ſelf had Mounted,
But that my Steed too weak I counted;
For my own Worth 'twould hardly bear,
Much leſs my Fellow-Traveller.
While thus my natural Benignity,
Beheld with Grief ſuch an Indignity,
And did againſt hard Fate difpute it,
Why *Bookſellers* ride, and *Authors* foot it;

Who

Who fhou'd I fee with all their Tackle
Within a Leathern Tabernacle
But Two, as Witty *S----* has it,
O'th' honefteft that e'er fold *Gazette*.
The Name o'th' Firft, but hold, let's pafs it;
The Second too fhall fecret be,
Left we fhould fpoil good Company.
They Hemm'd to my poor Militant Brother :
He heard, (for fharp are Ears of *Author*.)
Then took him up, and kindly carry'd
To Town in their Triumphant Chariot.
Me foon they fpy'd, as foon they beckon'd,
I joyn'd their Train, and made a Second.
On Converfation quickly fall,
Slap-dafh, And how, and how goes all ?
Who laft the *Athenians* did be-rogue Sir,
What *Auction*, or what *Catalogue* Sir ?
This idle News let's throw away,
And to the Bufinefs of the Day ;
Left we our Embryo-Notions fmother
With Gravity, fubjoins the other.

You know e're Fortune did convene us,
What was agreed upon between us;
That whofoe're a Project ftarted,
We'd both go halves, and have it parted.
Speak then, fince yet my Noddle won't ftir
And none that's here will us mifconfter
If any Prodigy or Monfter ;
Any rare glorious Fight or Murder
Of this fide *Tweed*, or on the further ;
For *Doeg's* Fuftian Quill to utter,
Doubly infpir'd with Bread and Butter.

C   Not

Not one of thefe my dear Acquaintance,
Who right or wrong ftill mind the Main-chance;
Not one good Whim, or I can't think on't,
Replies the firft, howe're let's drink on't:
How good Wits jump! The Thought they bleft,
Well-motion'd ftrait cry'd all the reft.
High did they heave the Courteous Bottle,
Transfus'd to Sympathetick Noddle,
Whofe Blood exhaufted, fills their Veins,
And crams Capacious Guts with Brains.
When one with Thanks to'th Juice that gave it,
Crys out, I have it Lads, I have it.
This very *Act*, altho 'twill many
Coft dear, with us fhall turn the Peny.
Whate're we lofe, we'll make Reprifal,
Whoever gains not, you and I fhall.

My very Thought, I'll fwear't fays t'other)
Howe're you came to hit on't Brother,
Bear witnefs elfe, *O'ambling Author*!
Say, did not I my felf propofe
This very Notion at the *Rofe*?

Poeta loqui-
tur.
Your're both my Friends, may Riches feize me
And make me dull, if I'd difpleafe ye:
Yet (as for Fibbing I defie it,)
'Twas the felf-fame, or very nigh it.
Howe're I'm fure you'll do a fair thing,
And ftand to your Authentick Bargain;
Your Servant's here to nick th'occafion
And give a Full and True Relation.

For that, crys he, if we find Stuff,
We can have Journey-Men enough.

Trade's

Trade's bad, Paper's too dear o'Confcience,
Nought fells befides th'*Athenian* Nonfence.
Oth' laft true *Bloody Fight* I printed,
In this own fruitful *Brain-pan* minted.
The *Hawkers*, which you'd fcarce believe,
Six Quire return'd me out of Five.
All this Sir not to beat you down ;
To Generous Souls what's Half a Crown ?
Below your Works intrinfick Value
No, by no means Sir wou'd we paul you :
We can be Civil Sir, you know it,
And we'll i'th' next *Edition* fhow it.
Nor for the firft will we be ftingy,
Or down to next to nothing dringe ye :
To hold you by the Teeth and Neck faft,
We'll give y'e a *Guinea* and a *Breakfaft* ;
Nay Brother, we'll that *Breakfaft* double,
Ne're ftand upon't but make't a Couple ;
Befides one Generous Pint to infpire him,
And for this high Atchievement fire him.
The other adds, well hang't, I'll take it,
And a rare piece ne're doubt on't make it.
I'll do my beft at Joque and Rallery,
Nor fear but 'twill, *Pit, Box* and *Gallery*.
Be each of you a careful Waiter,
An Eves-Dropper at the *Theatre*.
Come you but all well-laden home,
With *Thyme*, i'll work it into *Comb*.
He faid, and we by this were got over,
Thy Clowdy Brow, Sky-cliftring *Shot-over* ;
And juft as we had clos'd our twatling
O're *Maudlin-Bridge* the Wheels went ratling.
The Colledge felf's a little beyond,
You'll fee't next Door tot'h Sign of *Grayhound* :

Certainly fome Rogue or other muft print it upon him.

Poeta loquitur.

Shot-over-Hill.

Nor

Nor cou'd we much besides discover,
For now Dame Night came fluttering over :
Black Ghosts arose, and *Gown-Men* fled,
And *Tom* had warn'd the *Sun* to Bed.
Since for his *Exit*, vain's our Sorrow,
We'll Sleep, and tell you more to Morrow.

The End of the First Canto.

C A N T O.

CANTO II.

EXpect not our bold Mufe fhould call
The witty Moonfhine and the Wall,
To tell you what this Night betided,
Which knew no more than you and I did:
To leave then honeft *Townfmen* fnoring,
Some *Scholars* Tipling, others Whoring;
Some from th' intruding *Proctor* fcampring
T' avoid enchanted wooden Cramp-ring;
Or when that Cunning-Man has fpy'd 'em,
Charm'd by thofe powerful Words, *Per Fidem*;
Tripping away, without Bayardo,
Unto the *Caftle* or *Bocardo*,   *As much as*
As Rats are rim'd to fore Mifhap,   *to fay they*
And run their Heads into a Trap;   *go afoot thi-*
As Salt on Birds directly thrown   }   *ther.*
Probatum eft, their all they're own, }   *Similie.*
So here---But letting that alone.   }   *Similie.*
The Reader thinks as we intended
We'll here go on where laft we ended,
Comprizing in immortal Sing-Song
How all th' old Dons were at it Ding-dong.

         Their

Their Themes, the manner and occasion
Of every strenuous Disputation;
All this from point to point reciting,
And both his greedy Ears delighting.
Thus he, thus let him like a *Nisi*,
But we intend more to surprize ye,
To change the Scene, invert the Order,
Jogging in Road direct no further,
But with some Two or Three Supposes
Wiping our Gentle Reader's Noses;
Shall tell 'em all we did discover
Of this fam'd *Act*, as all were over;
As by good *Author* 'twas related,
The *Price* you know before debated:
And if he gives the secret Histories
Of any Scholar and his Mistress;
If Gown turn'd up he makes the wonder
At strange unheard Discoveries under,
We're not to answer for his Sawc'ness,
As knowing nothing of the Busi'ness:
Take Word for Word, from just Relators,
Not Paraphrasers, but Translators;
'Tis He, not we, are now to deal w'ye,
And so he pray'd me, Sirs, to tell ye.

The First rare Scene in this great *Drama*,
Was Mr. *Vice*'s grave *Pragramma*;
That all the *Lads* with Care exceeding
Should shew their *Haviour* and their *Breeding*;
On pain of *Black-Book* and the *Proctors*
Abusing none, besides the *Doctors*.

That those whom trembling *Soph* acknowledges
Right Worshipful of *Halls* and *Colledges*,
Should

Should fignifie to their Societies
During the *Act*, though now fo nigh it is,
All *Doctors* fhould their *Scarlet* wear,
As blufhing at the *Crimes* they hear.
And when the little Tingle-tangle
The Signal gives, prepare to wrangle.

All things and Places rightly ftated,
For *Graduates*, and *Non-graduated*.
For *Doctors*, *Mafters*, *Ladies*, *Fiddles*
The *Gall'ries* are referv'd ; the *Middle's*
Left open (Thanks,) for the *Rafcality*,
Servitors, and *Promifcuous Quality*.

Next the *Curators* muft take care
No breach of *Peace* be fuffer'd there ;
All with Decorum done, and Gravity,
No Rudenefs, or lewd Mob-like pravity :
The *Doctors*, as 'tis hop'd, abus'd,
The *Innocent Ladies* too mifus'd ;
Each little freedom there muft pocket,
Clap and Forgive th' ill-manner'd Blockhead.

And further, for the prefervation
Of *Alma Mater's* Reputation,
No *Scholar*, be he lefs or bigger,
Not Gown'd and Capp'd in Mood and Figure,
Muft have the Priviledge to hear
His Betters hift ith' *Theatre*.

Next fuch a Hift they could fupply it
From nothing but a *Polifh Diet* ;

Their

Their Names enough to have abafht one,
Legaffick, Strauchan and *Borafhton.*
The ftately *Perfian* Monarchs ufe
By length of Whiskers *Porters* chufe ;
So we our *Proctors* much the fame,
By Hardnefs, and by length of *Name,*

Tmefis. Who meet at One, that Mob may fear 'em,
I'th *Apo--* (what d'ye call't) *--dyterium.*

  Expect not I fhou'd make Relation
Of every Poem and Oration ;
The *Ladies* heard, (them I'll not flatter, or lie,)
And Edified moft fupernaturally :

Similie. As when St. *Tony* Preaching ftood
To's Four-Legg'd Brethren in the Wood.
Altho his Language was unwonted,
They cou'd not Hum, yet Thanks they grunted ;
Fain on their Maft wou'd had him Dine,
And prov'd themfelves all well-bred Swine.

  Now the full-button'd *Youth* appear,
And Squeaking, fill the *Theatre* ;
Their Parts well conn'd, fay over prettily,
Nay humour all things wondrous wittily.

  The prettieft littleft harmlefs Bawbles,
Young *Unfledg'd Lords,* and *Callow Nobles* ;
The *Ladies* might, nor wou'd they fcare 'em
For Nofegays in their Bofoms wear 'em ;
Not fo when Men of Parts and Converfe,
They've wit to fcorn---to write---their own Verfe.
Once harmlefs Worms, now fledg'd in Vices,
They're Bafilisks all, and Cockatrices ;

           Their

Their Mouths, their Eyes, their Tails difcover
Stings, Poifon, Murder, Death all over.
Yet honeft they perhaps continue,
Nor know they other ufe of *Guinea*,
But hungry *Poet* to requite
Who did their Gawdy Verfes write.
Who if he dares but claim his own,   }
When *Bully* meets him out of Town, }
Shot up to a Man, and ftrangely grown, }
With Valiant Whip he'll kindly Lace him,
Or elfe moft gratefully dry-bafte him.
Henceforth beware, dear Brethren, of it,
Take they the Honour, you the Profit:
Bought Wit is beft, and't has been faid for't,
It muft be theirs who fairly paid for't.
One fings, tho in Heroicks, odly
A Catalogue of the new *Bodley*:
While from another you may hear
Our fwinging the *French-Fleet*, laft Year.
A Third defcribes in lofty Fables
Their addled--*No-Defcent*----at *Naples*.
A Fourth fings *Britain's* Antient Glories,
Which the vile World will now think Stories.
A Fifth great *Ormonds* Praifes writes,
Heroically, as he Fights.
The next brave *Savoy's* long Recovering,
Who o're the *Gallick Foe* is hovering;
His Illnefs, how th'Allies deplore it,
And all he did, fince and before it.

But we had *Profe* as well as *Verfe* Sir,
Of which I'll be a true Rehearfer.

                How

How did the sharp *Inceptor Budgell*
His Holiness, and *Socinus* Cudgel ?
How *Tod* dispute, as sweet as Timbrel,
Of Schism and *Athanasian* Symbol?
How he who could in Egg-shell scribble
A General-Council prove fal-lible.
How *Bedford* talk at this great Season,
Of Fault, and Pain, and Light of Reason.
How *Brazan-Nose*, thy fam'd Entwistle,
Geneva and *Cracow* bids go whistle :
What *Cradock* the vain Deist say to
What he *de Opere Operato.*
What next of Royal *Christ-Church*, *Langford*
Which won't come in, tho I shou'd hang for't.
No more will any Physick-Question
Of *Sagittary* or of *Thurston* :
But Spirits and Piss, and Blood together
And Gout may go I care not whither.
Friend *à majori* proves, a Brute
Has Sense, because he can Dispute.
Brown will not let *Fanaticks* baffle us,
While *Prince* has power of *Adiapharous.*
Of *Kecking*, *Hannes* and *Salt's* Discourses,
And strange *Narcotick* Powers and Forces.
Last *Dale* affirms in sober Sadness
All great Wits have a spice of Madness,
Himself he'd for an Instance give 'em,
But is there any will believe him ?

    In this Employ the Day well worn,
They to the *Tennis-Court* adjourn.
A *Theatre*, tho far less spiteful
Than is their old, far more delightful ;

Where

Where the young *Lads* that never ventur'd,
Never 'till now, are fairly enter'd :
What there they do among the Wenches
Say, O ye Stools, O speak ye Benches :
Yet do not speak, your Voice would have us,
Like Vocal Head or Board 'twould scare us.

But *Luna* now is Heaven adorning,
So Friends adieu till the next Morning.

The End of the Second Canto.

CANTO III.

Use tell the Man, who like *Almanzor*
To every Mortal Wight crys Stand Sir ;
Discourteous Knight, whose Tongue dead-doing
Draws not for Ladies aid, but ruin :
Whether he *Terræ-Filius* height,
Or *Musick-Speech*, pronounce (not write,)
Midst Doctors, or their Wives is forraging,
His use, abuse, and Primitive *Origin*.   *Hysteron Proteron.*
But *Terræ-Filius* first invade,
And conjure up from Native Shade.

Have you not Read or Heard, Sir Reader,
Of an old *Grecian* Master Gard'ner ?   *Epicurus.*
Who that he might be fam'd for something,
Said, Man grew out of Earth, like Pumpkin ?
Ne're gern, and shew your Teeth, this Doctrin is
Embrac'd by th'Wits, and sage *Autochthones* ;
You some such Story, will ye, will ye,
Must own ith' Name of *Terræ-Filii* ;
Of Dunghil Race, and Education,
For strange Equivocal Generation :

Firm

Firm Proof you from their Birth may gather,
The Earth their Dam, the Sun their Father:
Hence, like their Brother *Dors* they rife,
And mean, but only mean the Skies:
When thofe in vain they've long affected,
Thither in vain their flight directed;
To Native Dirt, they fink forgotten,
By every Foot to nothing trodden.
The *Titans* firft of this lewd Race,
Which did ev'n Mother-Earth difgrace;
Proud big-bon'd, brainlefs, gracelefs Giants,
They *Jove* himfelf fet at defiance;
Who whirl'd his vengeful Thunder at 'em,
And funk 'em under *Styx* Ten Fathom.
This Mother *Terra* took fo ill
Th'Old *Crone* maintains the Quarrel ftill,
Was with new Rebel-Baftards gotten,
As foon as 'tother, dead and rotten:
With weaker Arms thefe Heaven affail'd,
The others Fought, thefe only Rail'd;
Their Malice-impotent began
With *Jove* himfelf, then each Good Man;
Old Comedy, and lawlefs Satyr,
Th'effect of Lewdnefs,' and Ill-Nature.
The Language was, which firft they fpoke in,
All Gravity and Virtue mocking:
They pleas'd to th' Life, the Mobs ill Natures,
Whofe Meat and Drink's to abufe their Betters;
This the true rife of all thy Scoffing is,
And fharp-edg'd Jefts, O *Ariftophanes*!
The Wittieft Knave we ever faw fince
The *Terra-Filius* of old *Athens*.
He with grave *Socrates* did fquabble,
And on him loo'd the grinning Rabble,
Abus'd the Doctor and his Wife,
Which coft the good Old Man his Life.
'Twou'd be too long to tell th'occafion
That brought 'em firft to th' Brittifh Nation;

And

And which oth' *Druids* did invite 'em
To *Beaumond*, alias *Bellositum*,
Who there of yore profefs'd Aftrology,
Sage Ethicks, Phyficks, and Theology ;
Which if you queftion, plain and liquid 'tis
Beyond difpute, in *Wood's* Antiquities ;
Afcetick-Wood's, whofe known good Nature,
So juftly curbs his harmlefs Satyr ;
Who takes fuch care on each occafion
To vindicate the Reformation :
None better cou'd fince or before do't,
Heylin or *Harmer* ne're did more do't.
Tho fome there are perhaps wou'd blame us,
For making their firft rife fo famous ;
And think thefe Under-Graduates-Oracles
Deduc'd from *Cornwal's* Givary Miracles,
From immemorial Cuftom there,
They raife a *Turfy Theatre* ;
Where from a Paffage under-Ground,
By frequent Crowds encompafs'd round,
Out leaps fome little Mephiftophilus,
Who ev'n of all the Mob the Offal is,
True *Terra-Filius* he, we reckon is,
Or *Anti-Theos Apomechanes* ;
Who Rimes, and Joques, and lays about him,
While Brawny Thoufands clap and fhout him.
Whence our new *Merry-Andrew's* Rife is,
Tranfplanted thence to Ford of *Ifis*.

And next the Mufe her Slave befeeches,
For a few Words of Mufick-Speeches ;
Whether from thofe old Strolling-Pedlers,
The Bawdy Corybantick Fidlers,
Who *Ifis* Temple oft had been in,
Not lov'd for nothing by the Women :
Or blind *Welch* Harpers, who for Farthings,
Told Tales, fung Songs, let F---s, fold Bargains.
We'll not difpute, fince there's no time for't,
Nor can we reafon find, or Ryme for't.

F   But

But to particulars defcending
To *Canto*'s hafte, and Poems ending.

But who alas ! who can fuffice,
Tho Tongues he had, like *Argus-Eyes*,
To tell of all the witty Rubs,
Spawn'd by who knows how many Clubs ?
Againft grave Doctors and fair Ladies,
As always at the Act the Trade is.
Sure there's a Letch'ry in Abufes,
They both have read *Flagrorum ufus*,
Tho an odd way, you'd think to move 'em,
The more their flogg'd, the more they love 'em.
Here the Wags maul one old *Sincater*, ⎫
Not *Hobbs* himfelf e're did it better ; ⎬
Whofe very Beard has found 'em matter ⎭
For Thirty Years Abufe and Satyr :
There generoufly another Hector,
And reverenced the poor Rector :
Not *Colmer* more, or great *T----*,
Him, or his Piece of Matrimony :
With Jeft fo eafie, all muft take it,
Of Gofpel, and of Woman Naked.
And fure, but him, none e're had knowledge
Of what is what in all the Colledge :
Not one of their Young Senior Fellows,
But's of his Chaftity fo jealous,
Should you a Naked Woman fhew 'em,
You'd fright 'em fo, 'twould quite undo 'em :
Put 'em beyond that fair occafion,
Beyond hot Cruft and Difputation,
Away, *Sans* Fear or Wit they'd fcamper,
In fpite of Ditch, of Wall or Rampire,
As Serpent, (fwallow't he that can,)
Fly from the fight of Naked Man.

Nor all is born by Doctors Backs,
For *Cambridge* too come in, for fnacks.

And

And is it thus, O ye *Oxonians*!　　　　⎫
Ye treat your Brother *Heliconians*,　　　⎬
The Christians, Jesuits, and the *Jonians* ?⎭
They'll fit you for't, and not be here,
'Till this time comes again next Year.

　　Next enter *Smith*, and very odd is't,
That he talks thus, the Chaft, the Modeft ;
See but with how much Grace he Blufhes,
At every Word all over Flufhes.
His Wit, his Modefty, or Learning ;
Whether's the moft needs deep difcerning,
His Wit, all rais'd by Contribution,
Or Military-Execution ;
For he fo neatly has exprefs'd it,
'Tis all his own, as he has drefs'd it.
His Modefty fure's more than common,
Since known to' above 500 Women :
At *Spencer*'s Squire of Dames he'd laugh,
Whom he out-throws a Bar and half.
Then for his Learning, 'tis notorious,
Made by his Modefty more glorious ;
But his chief Excellency is
As Envy own, in Languages ;
The *European* not enough,
The Modern only trifling ftuff,
With a far larger Scheme delighted,
All *Babels* are in him united.
What ever Traffiick brings from far
Indian, *Chinefe*, or *Malabar* ;
A natural *Hottamtot* he'd ape,
Deep vers'd it'h Language of the Cape ;
A happinefs fo ftrange and rare,
The Company fhou'd him prefer ,
Either to lie their *Leiger* there,
Or be at leaft Interpreter :
What near the Line, or near the Tropick,
Sclavonian be't, or *Ethiopick* ;
All, all's his own, he has no fmall fmattering,
Familiar-like, his *Greek* and *Latin* :

　　　　　　　　　　　　　　　Yes,

Yes, ev'n his *Greek* in which he'd have ye
To know, he'd out *Ariftotle's Davy.*
However he came by't, he'll teach ye
Scarce Satan more, what's Entelechy :
'Tis true, fuch Roots are often found
To thrive the beft in Barren Ground ;
But here's the wonder of the thing,
That they from fruitful Noddle fpring,
As full of Wit, by th' iffue all-may-fee,
As Aldermans of Senfe or Policy.
How plentifully this he fquander'd !
How neatly did he *Merry-Andrew't !*
Prick up your Ears to Repetion,
   Ladies, I am a bad Phyfitian ;
My Urinal I can produce ye,
And other Inftruments cou'd fhew t'ye,
By help of which there's none who better
Can caft or judge a Ladies Water :
I'm an Anatomift too and pleafe ye,
Of all the Female ails can eafe ye,
Not *Saffold* more, whofe Art I'nherit,
I the fole Heir of his Great Spirit.
But, be the Naked Truth confefs'd,
I'm at Man-Midwifery the beft.
Have you not heard of a Young Maiden,
Whom Modefty like mine, invading ;
When our lewd Sex, ours only were
Affiftants at the Groaning Chair ;
No Mortal having liberty
Without them to be born or dye ;
Finding befides they'd oft be fleering,
And their poor Female Patients jeering ;
Nay fometimes when they ought to bleed 'em,
Do fomething elfe, like Dr. *N----*
What does fhe but clap Foot in Stirrup,
Equipp'd with Breeches, Sword and Peruque ;
Till on a Stage good Fortune thanking,
A Quack fhe fpies a Mountibanking :
Patience fhe had fome half an Hour
To hear of Fam'd *Orvietan's* Power

Another half the Mob he aſſur'd,
What Crowds by others kill'd he had Cur'd :
And if there's any Females here
Who need a Father Confeſſor,
I'll not one Syllable diſcover,
But be as ſecret as a Lover.
Cure all their ails, tho ne'er ſo many,
Nor till perform'd, will ask a Peny.
Not as ſome Tinkering Doctors do
Who mend one Hole, by making too.
Ay here's the Man, the Virgin cry'd,
And to be ſhort, her ſelf appli'd
To Quack, deſiring if he's able
To teach this Skill ſo admirable ;
He did, ſince then, your Sex invaded
Our Art, nor with us longer Traded ;
But when you more than uſual yelp it,
Yes, thank ye, when you cannot help it.
Then gladly muſt you ſend agen
For me, or Doctor *Ch*---
For him at leaſt, ſince as for me
I come uncall'd, without a Fee,
Except a Drubbing on occaſion
Out of meer Superarrogation :
Diſguis'd leſt you my Beard ſhou'd gape on
With mighty Muffler, clean white Apron,
And cleaner Sleeves, I'm neat and ready,
With Eye like Eagle, Hand like Lady.
But one thing more, I ſhould have got me,
A Lions Heart, for your Anat'my.
That failing me, I quak'd and trembled,
My Ears and Tail in vain diſſembled.
The Aſs peep'd through and I was known,
And o're the curſt Balcony thrown.
Judge if my Skill not coſt me dearly,
Which at your Service is ſincerely,
T' anatomize on all occaſions
Your pretty Parts and Reputations.
No Favour or Affection ſhown,
Not your Sex only, but my own

G   Shall

Shall feel the dint of Musick-Speech,
And first have at *Lucretius---Gr*
Nor can there any thing be stranger
Than the occasion of my Auger.
Not that his first so well was done,
That Envy said 'twas not his own;
For some may so malicious be,
To say the same of this and me;
Nor that he's but a bad Translator
Of *Horace*, (tho pray shew me a better;)
But wot ye what's the very cause,
A curse upon his Lockram Jaws.
There was a Lady lov'd a Swine,
Preferring his sweet Face to mine;
Judge you, and if there's Justice in ye,
I dare shew with him for a Guinea.
Here's Eyes and Nose, here's Foot and Leg too,
To say no more of Shape and Neck too:
And him, yes him, O Times, O *Mores*,
To have that *Phiz* preferr'd before us!
That makes me fret as String of Fiddle,
And thus snap off my Tune i'th' middle.

That heap of Scandals I'll not write,
Which made for *Sm---* the Ladies Fight.
Tho other Lovers sure 'twould ruine,
At *Oxford* 'tis their way of woing.
So fair *Grimalkin* none espouses,
How well so e're th' old Gib-Cat Mouses ⎱
E're Musick-Speech's on the Houses; ⎰
And when they've pull'd each others Furr,
'Twill then be time enough to purr.
See how this Strokes, the other woes him,
That fain would lay in Lap or Bosom;
While back and forth he brushes by 'em,
With Tail on end, as he'd defie 'em.
Nor from each other need you guard 'em,
They'll not fight long, you need not part on.
With what you've heard, pray rest contented,
My *Book* and *Canto* here are ended.

F I N I S.

For Product Safety Concerns and Information please contact our EU representative GPSR@taylorandfrancis.com Taylor & Francis Verlag GmbH, Kaufingerstraße 24, 80331 München, Germany

T - #0058 - 270225 - C0 - 246/189/7 [9] - CB - 9780754630944 - Gloss Lamination